Focus on English
ESL Reference Series

Beyond Prepositions for ESL Learners Mastering English Prepositions for Fluency

by
Thomas Celentano

Third Edition 2017
Revised 2020

All inquiries should be addressed to: liaison@foebooks.com

A free audio version of this book can be found at https://foebooks.com/index.php/beyond-prepositions-for-esl-learners-audio/

Focus on English Books

10 9 8 76 5 4 3

Dedication

To my students everywhere

Forward

English prepositions are everywhere in the English language. The correct use of English prepositions in English communication can sometimes be difficult because of their unpredictable nature. This text was written as a quick reference guide, and primer, to help students quickly find and correct problem areas. The book was written for intermediate and advanced learners.

Notice to all students: a free audio version of this book can be found at https://foebooks.com/index.php/beyond-prepositions-for-esl-learners-audio/

Introduction

Focus on English© Mini Series Books
Making the difficult parts of learning English easy

Beyond Prepositions for ESL Learners - Mastering English Prepositions for Fluency

This book goes beyond just being a guide to the correct use of English prepositions. The student can use this text to learn how to correctly use prepositions, prepositional phrases, prepositions after certain English verbs, and prepositions in situational English communication in a wide variety of English sentence contexts. In addition to **complete and clear explanations** of the correct way to use prepositions, there are many **examples** of correct usage and **self reviews** throughout the book.

The student is encouraged to use this book in three ways:

- As a quick reference resource. The book layout and design make it easy for the student to quickly search for words or phrases of interest.

- As a learn-by-example text. Every step of the way there are many clear examples of usage, making it easy for the student to understand how English speakers use prepositions in everyday communication.

- As a grammar text. This book was designed to push the student to the next level in learning English prepositions in their many different

Thomas Celentano

usages. The practice and review sections of the book challenge the student to generate communication based on the lesson at hand, helping the student to reinforce his or her new knowledge.

Focus on English© Books for ESL Learners
Making the difficult parts of learning English easy

*Use **Prepositions** Correctly in Every English Sentence*

This book is designed for English Learners who want to clearly understand the use of prepositions in many different kinds of English sentences.

Why do English speakers say: a person gets <u>on</u> *a bus and* <u>into</u> *a taxi,* <u>on</u> *a plane and* <u>into</u> *a car; we arrive* <u>in</u> *New York* <u>at</u> *Kennedy Airport* <u>on</u> *Wednesday* <u>at</u> *3 p.m.* <u>in</u> *November; we sit* <u>at</u> *a desk but we sit* <u>in</u> *a chair; our hands are* <u>on</u> *the desk but our pencil is* <u>in</u> *our hand; we say we did something* <u>for</u> *him and then did something* <u>to</u> *him; I like my friend because he's* <u>like</u> *my brother; we have been talking* <u>about</u> *school* <u>since</u> *2 p.m.* <u>for</u> *3 hours* <u>outside</u> *the building that is* <u>close to</u> *the bank; the book is* <u>underneath</u> *the counter,* <u>beneath</u> *the bookshelf,* <u>under</u> *the window,* <u>near</u> *the door,* <u>beside</u> *the TV, which is* <u>next to</u> *the chair that is* <u>over</u> *the box that is* <u>on</u> *the floor . . . whew!*

Does some of this sound confusing to you? Well, don't worry! This Focus On English lesson is about English prepositions and will help you to understand and use English prepositions correctly in every situation.

How to use this preposition book

This book was designed to be both a reference book and a classroom text book that can be quickly searched for answers about the correct use of prepositions in most English sentences. At the end of this prepositions book there is an Appendix where the student can quickly find the correct prepositions that are used after certain English verbs.

"Prepositions Made Easy" is broken down into three sections.

The **first section** provides the student with the resources to understand the functional use of prepositions in everyday English communication. In this section, the student will find explanations and examples about how to use prepositions when talking about **time, place/location, transportation/travel, giving directions**, and **how things get done** (special uses for the prepositions <u>with</u> and <u>by</u>).

The **second section** is designed to help the student with the difficult area of prepositions following certain common verbs in English. The student may quick-search this second section easily, either by verb or by preposition, using the table of contents at the beginning of this book. This will save the student time and help to get answers quickly.

The **third section** is designed to be a reference resource for all of the most common prepositions used in English. This section contains a comprehensive listing of the prepositions followed by explanations and examples.

This book was designed to be used as a classroom study text or as a quick-search resource manual.

Table of Contents

Chapter 6 - Prepositions following verbs beginning with the letters <u>N</u>, <u>O</u>, <u>P</u>, and <u>Q</u> .... - 99 -

Chapter 7 - Prepositions following verbs beginning with the letters <u>R</u> and <u>S</u>.. - 105 -

Chapter 8 - Prepositions following verbs beginning with the letters T through Z

Section 3: Understanding the meanings and correct usage of all common English prepositions.............- 119 -

Chapter 1 - English prepositions beginning with the letters A̲ and B̲ ....- 120 -

Chapter 4 - English prepositions beginning with the letter O

Section 1: Using Prepositions correctly in context

 Learn to use English prepositions correctly when talking about time, places, transportation, giving directions, and expressing how things get done.

This first section helps the student to understand the use of English prepositions in real-life situations. In this section, the student will find explanations and examples relating to preposition usage in everyday English usage.

Chapter 1 - Using Prepositions to Talk About Time

Using the prepositions ***ahead***, ***behind***, ***at***, ***on***, ***in***, ***by***, ***within***, ***under***, ***during***, ***over***, ***since***, ***from***, ***for*** and ***after*** when talking about time in English

Directions: Read the brief explanations and then the examples below. *(Note: students are encouraged to use this text in groups, when possible. The student can then practice by listening and speaking, as well as reading, which should make learning easier, faster and more fun.)*

Ahead*:* Use ***ahead*** to talk about being earlier than expected   Delante de

Examples:

- The train is ***ahead*** of schedule. It was supposed to arrive at 9 a.m. but the time is now 8:55 a.m. and it is here!

- This is my first day of work, so I arrived at the office ***ahead*** of time.

  (Meaning: earlier than I was supposed to be there.)

Detrás de

Behind: Use **_behind_** to talk about being later than expected

Examples:

- The train is **_behind_** schedule. It was supposed to arrive at 9 a.m. but the time is now 9:05 a.m. and it's not here yet!.

- My watch says 12:30 p.m., but the time on the bank clock says 12:40 p.m. My watch must be **_behind_**.

In this case, meaning: the time on my watch lags the real time. English speakers also say: *my watch is slow*, or *my watch is running slow*.

En

_On_: Use **_on_** for day names, like Monday or Tuesday

Examples:

- My friends come to visit me **_on_** Wednesday.

- We have an important exam **_on_** Friday.

A tiempo

_On_: Use **_on_** in expressions like **_on_** time; **_on_** time means at the correct time or agreed upon time.

Example:

- My boss does not want me to come to work late. He wants me to come to work **_on_** time.

A

_At_ : Use **_at_** to talk about exact clock time.

Examples:

A la

- The exam will start **_at_** 3 p.m..

- The movie starts **_at_** 7:15 p.m..

At : Use **_at_** to talk about midnight, noon, night, daybreak, sunset, sunrise, etc.

Examples: *almuerzo*

- We had lunch **_at_** noon.

- We woke up **_at_** dawn (when the sun comes up).

- We went to bed **_at_** dusk (when the sun goes down).

_At_ : Use **_at_** in expressions referring to time: **_at_** the moment, **_at_** the present time, etc.

Examples:

- **_At_** the moment, doctors are not sure what causes cancer.

- **_At_** the present time, we are not hiring any more employees.

_In_ : Use **_in_** to talk about seasons of the year:

Examples: *En otoño*

- We will start school **_in_** the fall.

- Our vacation begins **_in_** the summer

_EN_

tiempo

_In_ : Use _in_ to talk about centuries, years, and months:

Examples:

- Cars were invented **_in_** the nineteenth century.

- We will finish class **_in_** May.

- We will graduate **_in_** 2012.

tiempo

_In_ : Use _in_ to talk about blocks of time:

Example:

- The woman said that she expects to have children **_in_** the future.

_In_ : Use _in_ to talk about named times of the day: morning, afternoon, and evening:

Examples:

- We have tea **_in_** the morning.   Por la mañana

- We eat lunch **_in_** the afternoon.   Por la tarde

- We have dinner **_in_** the evening.   Por la noche

_In_ : Use _in_ to talk about months of the year.

Example:

- I will complete my English course **_in_** February.

_In_ : Use _in_ to talk about years.

Example:

- I came to this country *in* 2001. *Eₙ 2001*

In : Use *in* in expressions like *in* time.

Example:

A tiempo para cenar

- He was just *in time* for dinner.

Justo a tiempo para cenar

    Meaning: he arrived when dinner was about to be served; at the correct time.

A tiempo

What is the difference between *in time* and *on time*? *In time* means that something has happened approximately at the same time as something else is happening or about to happen. Example: *We are about to have dinner, and you are just in time to join us.*

A tiempo

On time means that something has happened exactly at the agreed upon time. Examples: *The student was on time for school. School begins at 8 a.m. The student was on time.*

Example:

- He was *on time* for dinner. This means that he arrived at **exactly or near the time** when dinner was being served (just before, or exactly when dinner was being served)

Example using _in time_:

- We said dinner was at 6 p.m. and he arrived _in time_. This means that he arrived **sometime approximately around** the agreed upon time of 6 p.m..)

Dentro de una hora

Within : Use **_within_** to talk about something happening sometime inside of a specific timeframe.

Example:

- The bus should arrive **_within_** the next 15 minutes.

    Meaning sometime more than 1 minute and less than 15 minutes. So, for example, if it is 8 p.m., the bus should arrive sometime between 8 p.m. and 8:15 p.m. The bus is not expected to arrive at 8:15 p.m. exactly nor at 8 p.m. exactly, but some time in between these two times.

Debajo

Under : Use **_under_** when talking about something happening in less than a certain amount of time.

Example:

- I'm sure the train will be here in **_under_** an hour. (Meaning in less than an hour)

Sobre

Over : Use **_over_** when talking about something that takes more than a certain amount of time.

Examples:

✗ • I have been waiting here for you for ***over*** an
    hour.

✝ • The bus took ***over*** an hour to get to its next stop.

Durante

✗ **During** : Use ***during*** to talk about the time span in
which something happened.

Example:

• She cannot sleep well. She woke up several times
    during the night. (The time span was the
    nighttime hours when she was trying to sleep.)

Desde que

Since : Use ***since*** to talk about situations that
began in the past and continue to the present.

Example:

• I haven't felt well ***since*** I left my home country.

    Use since to refer to a specific time in the past
    like, for example, 1994 or 2 p.m.

For : Use ***for*** to talk about situations that began in
the past and continue to the present.

Continuar

Examples:

• I have been waiting here for the plane ***for***
    two hours.

- We have been taking this exam *for* 3 hours and I am tired.

Use for to talk about consecutive time like, for example, for 50 minutes or for 20 years.

From : Use **from** to talk about situations that will begin <u>now</u> or began at a certain time and continue into the future. *Ahora — —futuro*
now - futuro

Example:

- Last year we lost a very important soccer match to our rival. We were very sad. **From** that time on we never lost another game to our rival.

From that time on means *beginning* with that time and *continuing* into the future . . . .

By : When talking about time, use **by** to mean up to a certain time. —

Example:

- They will finish building our new house **by** next March.
  En un momento determinado

Practice - Using Prepositions When Talking About Time

Directions: Read the story below. Pay particular attention to prepositions _**at**_, _**on**_, _**in**_, _**by**_, _**within**_, _**under**_, _**during**_, _**over**_, _**since**_, _**from**_, _**for**_ and _**after**_. Let's begin:

I won the lottery!

Two weeks ago I won the lottery. I'm going to be rich! My life will change forever.

I've got an appointment with the lottery office _**at**_ 9 a.m. _**on**_ Wednesday. I'm going to the lottery office to pick up my $1,000,000 lottery prize!

**During** the telephone call, the person at the lottery office told me that I had to be at the lottery office _**on**_ January 5th, _**at**_ 9 a.m. That's _**on**_ a Wednesday. I haven't been able to sleep _**since**_ I learned that I won the lottery.

I have been waiting _**for**_ two weeks for this appointment. I want to buy many things.

I arrived at the lottery office _**at**_ 8:45 a.m. I was really nervous. The lady at the receptionist desk said that the lottery official would give me my prize money _**within**_ the next 15 minutes. I really hope he'll be here in _**under**_ 10 minutes because I am so excited about receiving this money.

During the time that I was waiting, it has been ***over*** five minutes now, I thought about that money. All that money! I was so excited. ***After*** today, I will be a rich person. I haven't had much money in my life. In fact, I have been poor ***for*** the last five years.

The secretary told me that I was the first person ***in*** the past three years, ***since*** 2005, to win $1,000,000.

I told her about my dream for the future: "***by*** next Wednesday," I said, "I want to have a new car, and ***in*** three years I want to have a home in Fiji."

I told the secretary: "I won't believe I really won the lottery ***until*** I receive the money in my hands."

Meanwhile, the lottery official opened his door and said, "I'll be out ***in*** five minutes."

I thought to myself: I will buy a brand new car ***by*** Monday, and, ***by*** Wednesday, I will buy a new apartment.

In fact, ***by*** the time you finish reading to this lesson, I will have received my money. I know what I'm going to do! The first thing I'm going to do after I get my money is buy a sailboat and sail around the world!

Quick Review - Using Prepositions When Talking About Time

Let's review the use of *on*, *at* and *in* for time sentences

Use *on* for day names, like Monday or Tuesday.

Use *on* in expressions like ***on time***.

Use *at* to talk about exact clock time. The exam will start *at* 3 p.m.

Use *at* to talk about midnight, noon, night, day, etc. For example: we had lunch *at* noon. We woke up *at* dawn. We went to bed *at* dusk (when the sun goes down).

Use *at* in expressions referring to time: *at* the moment, *at* the present time, etc. For example: *At* the moment, we are not sure what causes cancer.

Use *in* to talk about what will or may happen in the future: I will arrive *in* Tokyo *in* 4 days.

Use *in* to talk about seasons of the year. For example: we will start school *in* the fall. Our vacation begins *in* the summer

Use *in* to talk about centuries, years, and months. For example: cars were invented *in* the twentieth century. We will finish class *in* May. We will graduate *in* 2012.

Use *in* to talk about blocks of time. For example: I expect to have children *in* the future.

Use *in* to talk about named times of the day. For example: We have tea *in* the morning. We eat lunch in the afternoon. We have dinner in the evening.

Use *in* to talk about months of the year. For example: I will complete my English course *in* February.

Use *in* to talk about years. For example: I came to this country *in* 2001.

Use *in* in expressions like: *in* time. For example: He was just *in time* for dinner.

Snapshot - Using Prepositions When Talking About Time

What is the difference between *in time* and *on time*? *In time* means that something has happened approximately at the correct time. *On time* means that something has happened exactly at the right time.

He was *in time* for dinner. Means that he arrived at some time just before dinner was being served.

We said dinner was at 6 p.m. and he arrived *on time*. Means that he arrived exactly at 6 p.m.

Chapter 2 - Using Prepositions when Talking About Place or Location

 Using the prepositions ***above***, ***across***, ***after***, ***against***, ***along***, ***among***, ***around***, ***at***, ***below***, ***beside***, ***between***, ***beneath***, ***from***, ***in***, ***off***, ***on***, ***under***, and ***towards*** when talking about place or location.

Above : When talking about place, use ***above*** to mean something that is higher up than something else.

Examples:

- Oh look at that beautiful bird flying ***above*** our heads.

- The president is ***above*** all other managers in the company.

- The ceiling is ***above*** the floor.

Across : When talking about place, use ***across*** to express: from one side to the other.

Examples:

- The chicken walked ***across*** the street to eat some corn.

- The chicken walked ***across*** the busy street safely.

- The cruise ship sailed *across* the ocean to Europe.
- The man walked *across* the bridge to visit his secret lover.

After : Use *after* when talking about the 'next one' when talking about place or location.

Examples:

- The food store is the next building *after* the bank.
- The shopping mall is located on the next block *after* the high school.

Beside : Use *beside* when talking about something that is at the side of or next to something or someone.

Examples:

- The clothing store is *beside* the bank.
- The student sat *beside* the teacher while the teacher corrected his exam.

Against : When talking about place or location, *against* means something contacting or touching something else, pressing on it or pushing on it.

Examples:

- The woman leaned *__against__* the wall waiting for her boyfriend to meet her.

- The traffic was so bad that cars were almost *__against__* one another.

__Along__ : *__Along__* means over the length of something.

Example:

- The man walked *__along__* the busy road on his way to work.

__Among:__ *__among__* means something or someone in a group of people or things. There are usually more than two people or things in the group.

Example:

- The woman walked in the park *__among__* the flowers and trees.

Compare: She walked *__between__* two tall trees.

__Around__ : *__Around__*, first meaning: means in the immediate vicinity. Another way to say this is: something that is close by or near.

Example:

- The new hotel is *__around__* here, but we are not exactly sure where.

Around *:* ***Around****,* second meaning: when we talk about a place being on the other side of something (sometimes obscured from your view by something).

Examples:

- The bank is ***around*** the corner from here.

- The police station is ***around*** the other side of the building.

Around *:* ***Around****,* third meaning: moving here and there, randomly.

Examples:

- The couple walked ***around*** the neighborhood.

- The boy rode his bicycle ***around*** the town.

At *:* Use ***at*** to express being in front of, or up to something, but not in it.

Examples:

- He arrived ***at*** the train station ***at*** 3 p.m.. Compare this with: He went ***into*** the train station after he arrived.

- He was ***in*** the train station for 2 hours before his train arrived. The train took him to the airport.

- He was ***at*** the airport by 6 p.m.. He went ***into*** the airport to get his ticket. He was ***in*** the airport for 3 hours before his flight.

- The trash is kept **_at_** the back of the airport building.

_In_ : Use **_in_** to talk about your location within a city, state, country or other named political area.

Examples:

- I will arrive **_in_** Tokyo in 4 days. (Not **_at_** Tokyo)
- He arrived **_in_** New York on Wednesday.

Behind : **_Behind_** means at the back of or the rear of something or someone.

Examples:

- The trash is kept **_behind_** the building.
- The boy watched the house burn while his little sister hid **_behind_** him.

_On_ : Use **_on_** to talk about something in contact with or over a surface.

Examples:

- The book is **_on_** top of the desk.
- The book is **_on_** the desk.
- The picture is **_on_** the wall.
- The clock is **_on_** the wall.
- The map is **_on_** the wall.

- The light is **_on_** the ceiling.

Under, _beneath_ and _below_ : You can use **_under_, _beneath_ and _below_** in similar ways when you want to express something being physically lower than something else.

Examples:

- His feet are **_under_** the desk.
- His feet are **_beneath_** the desk.
- His feet are **_below_** the desk.

Practice - Using Prepositions when Talking About Place or Location

*Directions: Read and / or listen (if you are in a group) to this brief story about a college student named Tommy Morgan and his friends to help you further understand how the following prepositions are used: **above**, **across**, **after**, **against**, **along**, **among**, **around**, **at**, **below**, **beside**, **between**, **beneath**, **from**, **in**, **off**, **on**, **under**, and **towards**. After reading and / or listening you will be given some individual example sentences to practice with.*

Tommy Morgan and His Friends

Tommy Morgan sits **in** his chair **at** his desk. **On** his desk there is a book. **In** the drawer, **in** his desk, there are some school supplies like, for example, pencils and pens. His feet are **on** the floor **below** the desk and his hands are **above** the desk while his elbows rest **on** the desk.

His pen is **between** the pages of his book. His book is **on** his desk. His favorite pen is **among** the school supplies **inside** the drawer **in** his desk. His desk is located **in** the middle **of** the room.

Tommy Morgan wears very nice shoes **on** his feet. **In** his right hand there is a pencil. His teacher sometimes tells him he should take his hat off. So he takes his hat off and puts it **under** the chair where he sits. His friend Mary sits in front of him **at** her desk. His friend Hiro sits _**at**_ the desk _**at**_ the back of the room. His friend Julio sits _**at**_ the desk _**behind**_ Tommy.

Today, the teacher is talking to the students about English grammar. _**At**_ the top _**of**_ the whiteboard, the teacher wrote three irregular verbs. _**At**_ the bottom _**of**_ the whiteboard the teacher wrote three regular verbs. The teacher asks Tommy to come _**to**_ the white board and write a sentence for each verb. She asks him to write the sentences _**in**_ the middle of the whiteboard. Tommy leaned _**against**_ the whiteboard and thought for a moment. Then he began to write his sentences _**in**_ the middle of the whiteboard.

**Across from** the university, there is a pub. The pub is _**on**_ the corner of Warren Avenue and Jackson Place. _**On**_ Friday nights, Tommy, Hiro, Julio and Mary meet _**at**_ the pub. Mary asked Hiro, "where is the new restaurant that you told me about?' Hiro answered, "I'm not sure, I read about it in the newspaper; it's _**around**_ here, not too far away." Mary replied, "oh, so the restaurant is near the pub. Let's go to the restaurant after we go to the pub."

Inside the pub everyone was having a great time. They went _**into**_ the pub and had such a good time that they stayed there _**for**_ four hours and forgot their idea about going to the restaurant!

Review and Practice - Using prepositions when talking about location or place

Directions: Read and / or listen carefully to the sentences below. Fill in the blanks using one of the following prepositions: **above**, **across**, **after**, **against**, **along**, **among**, **around**, **at**, **below**, **beside**, **between**, **beneath**, **from**, **in**, **off**, **on**, **under**, and **towards**. The answers can be found in this chapter (above).

1. Oh look at that beautiful bird flying _____ our heads.

2. The ceiling is _____ our heads.

3. The man walked _____ the street to visit his secret lover.

4. Wal-Mart is the next building _____ the bank.

5. Wal-Mart is _____ the bank.

6. The woman leaned _____ the wall waiting for her boyfriend to meet her.

7. The man walked _____ the busy road on his way to work.

8. The woman walked ____ the park among the flowers and trees.

9. The new hotel is _____ here, but we are not exactly sure where.

10. The couple walked _____ the neighborhood.

11. He arrived ___ the train station at 3 p.m.

12. He arrived ___ New York *on* Wednesday.

13. The businesswoman is *in* the car. The man got ____ the train and then ____ a plane to New York.

14. We arrived *at* the train station ____ 2 p.m. Then we went inside the train station. We were *in* the train station when our train arrived ___ 3 p.m.

15. The chicken walked _____ the busy street safely.

16. The trash is kept _____ the building.

17. The trash is kept ___ the back *of* the building.

18. The book is ___ top *of* the desk. The book is *on* the desk

19. His feet are _____ the desk. His feet are *beneath* the desk. His feet are *below* the desk.

Answers: (1) above; (2) above; (3) across; (4) after or beside; (5) beside; (6) against; (7) across; (8) around or in; (9) around; (10) in or around; (11) at; (12) in; (13) on . . . on; (14) at . . . at; (15) across; (16) beside or against; (17) at; (18) on; (19) under

Chapter 3 - Using Prepositions when Talking About Transportation and Traveling

Using the prepositions _**in**_, _**on**_, _**at**_, _**into**_, _**off**_, _**across**_, _**from**_-_**to**_, _**along**_ and _**between**_ when talking about transportation and traveling

_On_: Use **_on_** to talk about trains, buses, and planes. (Contrast with **_in_**.)

Examples:

- I got **_on_** the bus to go to the center of the city.
- When we got **_on_** the plane, we had a difficult time finding our seats.
    - We got **_on_** the train just in time; the train was about to leave.
    - The man got **_on_** the train and then **_on_** a plane to New York.

Using _in_ and _inside_ note: it _is_ true that you are inside the bus, train or plane when you are traveling, but English speakers say "I'm **_on_** a bus to Seattle", for example, if someone calls them on their cell phone.   It is more common for English speakers to use **_in_** or **_inside_** when talking about public transportation, for example, when they are talking about things that may have happened while they were traveling, or things that were observed inside the transportation vehicle.

Examples:

- There was a lot of noise *inside* the bus while we were going home.

- All of the passengers *in* the plane were enjoying the movie.

- The lights *in* the train were very bright.

_In_ and _Into_ : Use *in* and *into* to talk about taxis, cars and limousines.

Examples:

- The businesswoman left her house at 10 p.m. and then got *into* her car and drove to work.

- The two students waved at the taxi to stop.

- When the taxi stopped, they got *in* and told the taxi driver where they wanted to go.

_By_ : Use *by* to talk about how you traveled; what form of transportation.

Examples:

- The family traveled *by* plane to Beijing.

- The boy went to school *by* foot.

- The businesswoman traveled to Frankfurt **_by_** train.

- We went to the movies **_by_** bike.

Off : Use **_off_** in the phrasal verb, **_to get off_**, to talk about disembarking and arriving at a destination.

Examples:

- The businessman took the train to New Jersey and **_got off_** in Newark.

- We are taking a plane to Dallas but we are **_getting off_** in Reno, Nevada.

(Note: Don't use **_get off_** when referring to a taxi, car, or limousine (for example, don't say "I got off the taxi") Use **_get out of_** or **_arrived in_** a taxi, car or limousine. For example: I arrived in New York **_in_** a taxi. I **_got out_** of the taxi, paid the taxi driver, and went **_inside_** the train station to catch the next train to Philadelphia.)

Between : Use **_between_** to talk about distance from one location to another location.

Example:

- What is the distance **_between_** New York and Los Angeles? Oh, it's about 2400 miles.

From - to : Use **_from - to_** to talk about travel plans or distance **_from_** one location **_to_** another location.

Example:

- How long does it take to travel **_from_** New York **_to_** Chicago?

- The distance **_from_** Seattle, Washington **_to_** Atlanta,

- Georgia is about 2,900 miles.

- Could you tell me how to get **_to_** St. Peters Cathedral **_from_** here.

Along : Use **_along_** to talk about traveling over a length of road or train track.

Example:

- We took a train to Miami, Florida. As we traveled **_along_** the tracks, we could see many farms.

Practice and Review - Using Prepositions
when Talking About Transportation and Traveling

Directions: *Read this brief story about an English
student named Sonya as she travels for the first time in
the United States. Read and / or listen carefully to how
prepositions are used to talk about transportation and
traveling. Fill in the blanks with the correct preposition.
Answers are at the end of the chapter.*

Sonya's first trip to Seattle

Sonya came to the U.S. last year to study English (1)
_____ New York. She arrived ***in*** New York (2) ___ May
30th. After studying English ***in*** New York, she decided
to travel ***across*** the United States using ground
transportation like trains, buses, and taxis so that she
could see what America looked like.

(3) _____ New York, she decided to take a train ***to***
Cleveland, Ohio. On the day that she decided to leave,
she got (4) _____ a taxi in front of her hotel and told the
driver to take her to the railroad station. When she
arrived ***at*** the railroad station she got ***out*** of the taxi, paid
the driver, and went (5) _____ the train station.

After she bought her ticket ***at*** the ticket counter, she
waited ***inside*** the train station for over an hour, until her
train arrived.

When the train arrived and opened its doors, Sonya got
(6) _____ the train and found a nice seat ***by*** the window.

She took many pictures *from* her window seat during the ride to Cleveland. The train was scheduled to stop (7) ___ Pittsburgh, Pennsylvania and Alliance, Ohio before continuing on to Cleveland. When the train stopped *in* Pittsburgh, Sonya got (8) ____ to have a quick look around.

After getting (9) ___ the train again, Sonya had some dinner. As the train traveled (10) _____ the tracks, the sun was going down. Sonya is going to arrive in Cleveland at dusk, just in time to find a hotel room for the evening.

Answers: (1) in ; (2) on ; (3) In ; (4) in ; (5) into ; (6) on ; (7) in ; (8) out ; (9) on ; (10) along

Chapter 4 - Using Prepositions when Giving Directions

Using the prepositions _**in**_, _**on**_, _**at**_, _**near**_, _**down**_, _**towards**_, _**across**_, _**from**_, _**between**_, _**around**_ and _**among**_ when talking about giving directions

Using prepositions when giving directions

**Towards** : When giving directions, use _**towards**_ to mean in the direction of something.

Example:

- Could you please tell me how to get to the bank?

  Sure. Walk down this street _**towards**_ the fountain in the center of the city. Turn left at Warner Street.

_**In**_ : When giving directions, use _**in**_ to mean inside of an area or boundary:

Example:

- Could you please tell me how to get to the bank?

  Sure. Walk down this street _**towards**_ the fountain _**in**_ the center of the city. Turn left at Warner Street and you will see the bank on your right, _**in**_ the financial district.

_On_ : When giving directions, use _on_ with street, road or highway to indicate location; or use _on_ in expressions like _on the right_.

Example:

- Could you please tell me how to get to the bank?

  Sure. Walk down this street towards the fountain in the center of the city. Turn left at Warner Street and you will see the bank **_on_** your right, in the financial district. It's **_on_** Warner Street near Sunrise Road.

Near _:_ When giving directions, use _near_ to mean close to.

Example:

- Could you please tell me how to get to the bank?

  Sure. Walk down this street towards the fountain in the center of the city. Turn left at Warner Street and you will see the bank on your right, in the financial district. It's on Warner Street **_near_** Sunrise Road.

Across : When giving directions, use _across_ to mean from one side to the other side:

Example:

- Could you please tell me how to get to the bank?

Sure. Walk down this street towards the fountain in the center of the city. Turn left at Warner Street and you will see the bank on your right, in the financial district. It's on Warner Street near Sunrise Road. You may need to walk ***across*** the street. It's ***across*** from the library and between the food store and the computer store.

At: When giving directions, use ***at*** to indicate the location of something

Example:

- Could you please tell me how to get to the bank?

  Sure. From here, walk down this street towards the fountain in the center of the city. Turn left ***at*** Warner Street and you will see the bank on your right, in the financial district. It's on Warner Street near Sunrise Road. You may need to walk across the street. It's across from the library and between the food store and the computer store. There are some trees growing at the front of the bank building. The bank is around the corner from the new park.

Around: When giving directions, use ***around*** to talk about something being close, or something located on the other side of something else.

Example:

- Could you please tell me how to get to the bank?

  Sure. From here, walk down this street towards the fountain in the center of the city.

  Then, turn left at Warner Street and you will see the bank on your right, in the financial district.

  It's on Warner Street near Sunrise Road. You may need to walk across the street.

  It's across from the library and between the food store and the computer store.

  There are some trees growing at the front of the bank building. The bank is ***around*** the corner from the new park, ***around*** where the library is.

Practice and Review - Using Prepositions when Giving Directions

Let's read again the discussion about finding the bank. Pay attention to the prepositions and how they are used. See if you can fill in the blanks with the correct answers.

Could you please tell me how to get to the bank?

Sure. **_From_** here, walk **_down_** this street **_towards_** the fountain (1) ___ the center **_of_** the city. Turn left (2) ___ Warner Street and you will see the bank **_on_** your right, **_in_** the financial district. It's **_on_** Warner Street **_near_** Sunrise Road. You may need to walk (3) _____ the street. It's **_across_** **_from_** the library and **_between_** the food store and the computer store. There are some trees growing **_at_** the front of the bank building. The bank is (4) _____ the corner **_from_** the new park, **_around_** where the library is.

Answers: (1) in ; (2) on *or* at ; (3) across ; (4) around

Chapter 5 - Using with and by to Express
How Things are Done

 Below we will discuss these important prepositions and provide you with many examples. If you are working in a group, listen carefully to the pronunciation of these expressions in complete sentences.

Some examples of using **_with_** and **_by_** to express how things are done:

- The beautiful dress was made **_by_** hand. Katrina made the beautiful dress **_with_** her own hands.

- The construction worker dug the hole **_by_** hand (meaning: manually, with a shovel in his hands; without the help of a machine).

- The construction worker dug the hole **_with_** his hands (meaning manually, without a shovel or the help of a machine; using his own two hands).

- The family traveled to South Africa **_by_** air. We sent the letter **_by_** airmail. We went to school every day **_by_** foot.

- We walked into the wrong room **_by_** mistake.

- We paid for the meal **_with_** a check. We paid for the meal **_by_** check. We paid for the meal **_in cash_**.

- We were lucky; _**by**_ chance we found the examination room right before the exam was going to begin.

Some rules and examples for using _with_ and _by_:

_**By**_: _By_ is used to talk about the way you travel or how you travel.

Examples:

- I go to work _**by**_ bus.
- I went to Europe _**by**_ plane.

_**By**_: _**By**_ is used to talk about how you communicate or send mail or packages.

Example:

- We talked _**by**_ phone.
- We sent the package to India _**by**_ airmail.
- My friend and I communicate _**by**_ email.

_**By**_: _**By**_ is also used in expressions like: _**By mistake**_ (meaning: to do something in error) and _**by check**_ (meaning: a method of payment)

Example:

- I dialed the wrong number ***by mistake***. I apologized to the person who answered the phone.

- I often pay my bills ***by check***.

Note: if you pay for something with cash, we often say '***in cash***'.

Examples:

- I paid for the new car ***in*** cash.

- I paid the bill ***in*** cash.

It is also possible to say ***with cash***.

Example:

- I paid for the tickets ***with*** cash.

By chance: something that happens that is not planned; luckily or unluckily

Example:

- ***By chance***, the dress was on sale when we arrived at the shop. We didn't expect to find the dress on sale.

By choice: someone's decision or preference to act in a certain way; a decision originating from one's own free will

Example:

- **_By_** choice, I am single (not married)

  (meaning I choose not to be married).

_By_ : Using **_by_** plus a gerund. Use **_by_** plus a gerund to express a method of doing something

Example:

- I sent an email **_by_** press**_ing_** the send button.
- I repaired the car **_by_** adjust**_ing_** the engine.

With: Use **_with_** when you are talking about using something like a tool or an instrument to do something, or when you are talking about using some part of your body to do something.

Examples:

- I fixed the engine **_with_** a wrench.
- I kicked the door **_with_** my foot.
- I sewed the clothing **_with_** a needle

Let's Practice and Review - Using the Prepositions *by* and *with*

*Read the following story and fill in the blanks with either **by** or **with**. Answers can be found below.*

1. My friend Jaime and I decided to travel to Hawaii for our vacation. We knew that the flight _____ plane was going to be a long one from Europe, but we really wanted to go to Hawaii.

2. Before we bought tickets, we decided to contact our travel agent in Barcelona (a)_____ email to get more information about travel to Hawaii. By chance, out travel agent was working (b)_____ her computer when our email arrived, and she answered our email quickly.

3. She answered our email (a) _____ telling us that she would be happy to give us a brochure about travel to Hawaii. She said that it was probably a good idea to bring a credit card because paying for everything (b) _____ cash was not practical, and it would be dangerous to walk around (c)_____ lots of cash in our pockets. Paying (d) _____ personal check was not a good idea either because many stores in Hawaii do not accept checks that are not from a local bank in Hawaii. She said that going to Hawaii (e)_____ Traveler's Checks was a good idea because merchants

accepted these in the same way that they accept cash and they were safe to carry in our pockets.

4. When we arrived in Hawaii, we traveled (a)___ bus from the airport to our hotel room. During the ride from the airport we could see Hawaii's beautiful beaches and parks. It smelled like the air was filled (b)_____ flowers, and it was warm and the sky was very blue.

5. The bus let us off in front of a group of hotels (a)_____ all of our luggage. (b)___ mistake, we walked into the wrong hotel. When we asked the clerk at the desk about our reservation, the clerk said that our names were not on the list.

6. ___ chance, there was another person standing at the counter who offered to help. He looked at our itinerary and quickly helped us to find our hotel, which was right next door. He walked with us a little so he could point to the hotel.

7. After getting settled in our hotel room, the rest of the vacation in Hawaii was very exciting. We went ___ bus to see the island.

Answers: (1) by; (2) (a) by; (b) with ; (3) (a) by; (b) with ; (c) with ; (d) by (e) by; (4) (a) by: (b) with ; (5) (a) with (b) by; (6) by; (7) by

Mastering English Prepositions

Section 2: Using Prepositions Correctly After Certain Common English Verbs

Learn to use English prepositions correctly after certain commonly used English verbs.

English has many important expressions that use a combination of verbs plus prepositions or adjectives (beginning with the "be" verb plus prepositions).

How do you know which preposition to use after these verbs? Well, there are no set rules for this. But don't worry! This Focus On English section will help you to understand and then practice and master using these verb-preposition combinations correctly.

Chapter 1 - Prepositions Following Verbs Beginning with the Letter A

In this chapter you will find the English verbs, beginning with the letter 'a,' that are commonly followed by prepositions. An explanation of the verb / preposition combinations is followed by examples of how English speakers typically use these in a wide variety of English sentences.

There are no set rules that might help you to understand which preposition follows a variety of common English verbs. So here you will find the English verbs that are commonly followed by prepositions. Verb / preposition combinations are followed by some examples of how English speakers typically use these in a wide variety of English sentences.

Using prepositions in expressions with certain verbs Verbs beginning with the letter A

Using prepositions in expressions with certain verbs - verbs beginning with the letter A

To be **absent from**:

Examples:

- Students should not **_be absent from_** class.

- Alex **_was_** not **_absent from_** the meeting.

To **_be accustomed to_** (something or someone): similar in meaning to *be used to*

Examples:

- The girl **_is accustomed to_** shopping at the store near her house.

- Kaori **_is accustomed to_** walking home from school.

To be **_acquainted with_** (something or someone):

Examples:

- I **_am acquainted with_** that man. He is the one who brought the package to our house.

- We **_were acquainted with_** the school's rules because we went to an orientation.

To **_admire for_** (something or someone):

Examples:

- I **_admire him for_** getting a high grade on his exam.

- Gina **_admired her mother for_** getting a university degree.

To be **_afraid of_** (something or someone):

Examples:

- I **_am afraid of_** walking home alone in the dark.

- Lucy **_is afraid of_** swimming in the ocean.

To **_agree with_** (something or someone)

Examples:

- I **_agree with_** my friend. We both have the same opinion about politics.

- Sally **_agreed with_** her advisor when her advisor told her she should change jobs.

To be **_ashamed of_** (something or someone)

Examples:

- I **_am ashamed of_** my friend for stealing the car.

- Clarence **_was ashamed of_** the bad grade that he got on the exam.

To be **_amazed at_** or **_by_** (something or someone)

Examples:

- I **_am amazed at_** how hard he studied for that exam; almost five hours every night!

- The crowd **_was amazed at_** the circus act.

To be *angry at* or *with* (something or someone)

Examples:

- I *am angry with* / *at* my girlfriend for not telling me she was dating someone else.

- The tourists were angry *with* / *at* the tour guide for speaking too quickly.

To *apologize for* (doing something wrong) or *to* (something or someone)

Examples:

- I *apologized* to the teacher *for* being late. I *apologized for* being late.

- The policeman *apologized* to his boss *for* arresting the wrong person.

To *apply to* or for

Examples:

- I *applied to* the school for admission. I *applied for* admission.

- Sam *applied for* a new job.

To *approve of* (something or someone)

Examples:

- My company ***approves of*** the way I dress when I come to work.

- The passengers on the plane ***approved of*** the way the stewardess did her job.

To ***argue with*** (something or someone)

Examples:

- I ***argued with*** my boss about the project deadline.

- She ***argued with*** her mother about staying out past 10 p.m..

To ***arrive at*** or ***in*** (*at* a location / building; *in* a city or country)

Examples:

- I ***arrived at*** school at 8 a.m.. She will ***arrive in*** the United States on Wednesday.

- The hockey team ***arrived at*** the arena at 4:30 p.m..

To ***ask for*** or ***about*** (something or someone)

Examples:

- I ***asked*** him ***for*** a pencil.

- I ***asked*** her ***about*** the exam that she took yesterday.

- The little boy ***asked*** his grandpa ***for*** some candy.

To be **_aware of_** (something or someone)

Examples:

- He **_is aware of_** the penalty for breaking the law.
- We **_were aware of_** the high prices before we entered the store.

To be **_awful at_** (something or someone)

Examples:

- He **_is awful at_** cooking. It's lucky that he has a wife that can cook.
- She **_is awful at_** drawing pictures. She's better at writing.

Let's Practice and Review

Read the following sentences and fill in the blanks with the correct preposition. Answers can be found below.

1. Our boss *__approves__* _____ the way we completed the report.

2. James *__asked__* his teacher _____ the exam yesterday.

3. My friend *__agrees__* _____ me.

4. I *__am ashamed__* _____ our team for losing so badly.

5. I *__admire him__* _____ being brave during the match.

6. Sally *__is afraid__* _____ walking home alone in the dark.

7. Tricia *__is accustomed__* _____ riding the bus home from school.

8. Four students were *__absent__* _____ school.

9. Jim *__was angry__* _____ his girlfriend for not telling him that she was dating someone else.

10. The tourists *__were amazed__* _____ how big the building was.

11. The student *__applied__* ____ the school for admission.

12. I *__apologized__* _____ the bus driver *__for__* my extra baggage.

13. Jackie *__argued__* _____ her boss about the new project.

Answers: (1) of; (2) about; (3) with; (4) of ; (5) for; (6) of; (7) to ; (8) from; (9) at; (10) at; (11) to; (12) to; (13) with

Chapter 2 - Prepositions Following Verbs
Beginning with the letters B and C

Using prepositions in expressions with certain verbs – beginning with the letters B and C

To be **_bad for_** (something or someone)

Examples:

- Smoking **_is bad for_** your health.
- Factory pollution **_is bad for_** the environment.

To **_believe in_** (something or someone)

Examples:

- I **_believe in_** good luck.
- The people **_believed in_** its government.

To **_belong to_** (something or someone)

Examples:

- The pen **_belongs to_** me.
- The sports car **_belongs to_** the movie star.

To be **_bored with_** or **_by_** (something or someone)

Examples:

- I'm ***bored with*** working every day.

- I'm ***bored by*** that TV show. Can we change the channel?

To ***borrow*** something ***from*** (something or someone)

Examples:

- Tommy Twoshoes ***borrowed*** $10 ***from*** Julio.

(Julio ***lent*** $10 to Tommy Twoshoes.)

- Alicia ***borrowed*** Jim's bicycle ***from*** him.

To be ***careful of*** (something or someone)

Examples:

- ***Be careful of*** the fast-moving cars when you cross the street!

- Calvin told me to ***be careful of*** drinking tap water when traveling.

To ***compare to*** or ***with*** (something or someone)

Examples:

- When I ***compare*** swimming ***with*** (***to***) running, I think that swimming is more difficult.

- ***Compared to*** our team, the opponent's team looks weak.

To ***complain to*** or ***about*** (about something or someone)

Examples:

- I ***complained to*** my teacher ***about*** the cold air conditioning in the room.

- Ginger ***complained about*** the bad food in the restaurant.

To be ***composed of*** (something)

Examples:

- Coke a Cola ***is composed of*** (made of) mostly sugar.

- Bread ***is composed of*** mostly flour.

To ***concentrate on*** (something or someone)

Examples:

- The student has an exam the next day so he ***concentrated on*** studying.

- The athlete ***concentrates on*** winning.

To be ***concerned about*** (something or someone)

Example:

- She *__is concerned about__* her weight. She is gaining weight.

- His parents *__were concerned about__* his poor grades in school.

To *__consist of__* (something) (meaning: made up of certain ingredients)

Examples:

- A good meal *__consists of__* fish, vegetables and rice.

- A good report *__consists of__* lots of research and hard work.

To be *__content with__* (something or someone) (meaning: to be happy with)

Examples:

- The quiet, simple man *__is content with__* his life.

- Amy *__is content with__* her new car.

To be *__crazy about__* (something or someone)

Example:

- She *__is crazy about__* ice cream. She really likes to eat ice cream.

- She'*__s crazy about__* her boyfriend.

To be ***curious about*** (something or someone)

Examples:

- The customer ***was curious about*** the price of the car.

- The police detective ***was curious about*** the blood on the floor.

Let's Practice and Review

Read the following sentences and fill in the blanks with the correct preposition. Answers can be found at the bottom of this page.

1. The red Ferrari **_belongs_** _____ me.

2. Fiberglass **_is composed_** _____ silica fibers.

3. The student **_was curious_** _____ the cost of the textbook.

4. Good Italian pasta sauce **_consists_** _____ tomatoes, garlic, olive oil, and seasoning.

5. His father **_was concerned_** _____ the cost of a new roof for his house.

6. The children **_believe_** _____ magic.

7. Drinking too much alcohol **_is bad_** _____ your health.

8. Tim Evans **_borrowed_** $20 _____ Hiro.

9. **_Be careful_** _____ the snake on the ground right next to you!

10. Jenny **_complained_** _____ her teacher _____ the noise in the next room.

11. My friend _**compared**_ his car _____ mine and decided to buy a new car.

The swim team _**concentrated**_ _____ learning better techniques.

Chapter 3 - Prepositions Following Verbs Beginning with the letters **D** and **E**

Using prepositions in expressions with certain verbs – beginning with the letters D and E

Using prepositions in expressions with certain verbs - verbs beginning with the letters D and E

To **_depend on_** (something or someone)

Examples:

- Car motors **_depend on_** gasoline or diesel fuel to run.

- She **_depends on_** her friends for help with her homework.

To be **_devoted to_** (something or someone; to be loyal to)

Examples:

- She **_is devoted to_** her husband.

- The professor **_is devoted to_** his research.

To be **_different from_** (something or someone)

Examples:

- Coffee ***is different from*** tea.
- Apples ***are different from*** oranges.

To ***disagree with*** (something or someone)

Examples:

- I ***disagreed with*** him about smoking in the classroom.
- The lawyers ***disagreed with*** each other in court.

To be ***disappointed in*** (something or someone)

Examples:

- I ***was disappointed in*** our team. They lost the game.
- Jenny ***was disappointed in*** the quality of the fruit at the market.

To ***discuss*** (something) ***with*** (someone)

Examples:

- I ***discussed*** the problem ***with*** my boss.
- The students ***discussed*** the assignment ***with*** the teacher.

To ***divide into*** (divide something into)

Examples:

- I **_divided_** the cake **_into_** two pieces so my friend could have some.

- The manager **_divided_** the workers **_into_** three groups.

To be **_divorced from_** (something or someone)

Examples:

- The woman **_was divorced from_** her husband.

- They **_have been divorced from_** each other for two years.

To **_dream of_** (something or someone)

Examples:

- She **_dreamed of_** going to the South Pacific for a vacation.

- The couple **_dreamed of_** having their own house in the future.

To be **_engaged to_** (someone)

Examples:

- The man and woman **_were engaged to_** each other. They planned to get married in one month.

- Alex and Cynthia **_were engaged to_** each other in March, but broke off the engagement in April.

To be ***equal to*** (something or someone)

Examples:

- His English skills ***are equal to*** her English skills.

- The two soccer teams ***are equal to*** each other in match records.

To ***escape from*** (something or someone)

Examples:

- The prisoner ***escaped from*** prison and the police cannot find him.

- The young dog ***escaped from*** the cage and ran away.

To be ***excited about*** (something or someone)

Examples:

- I ***am excited about*** my summer vacation. I am going to Asia.

- We ***are excited about*** going to Hawaii.

To ***excuse*** (someone) ***for***:

Examples:

- My boss ***excused*** me ***for*** being late for work.

- Frank ***excused*** his friend ***for*** not wanting to go on the hike.

To be _**exhausted from**_ (something)

Examples:

- I _**was exhausted from**_ working in the garden all day.

- Our team _**was exhausted from**_ playing so hard in the competition.

Let's Practice and Review

Read the following sentences and fill in the blanks with the correct preposition. Answers can be found at the bottom of page.

1. I **_divided_** the cake _____ five pieces so all of my friends could have some.

2. Our team lost. I **_was_** really **_disappointed_** _____ our team.

3. We **_discussed_** the plan _____ our superior.

4. The players **_disagreed_** _____ the referee.

5. Monty **_is devoted_** _____ playing the violin.

6. Airline pilots **_depend_** _____ ground control to help them land safely.

7. Surfing **_is different_** _____ snow boarding.

8. My brother **_dreamed_** ___ becoming an engineer.

9. Toby's grades **_are equal_** _____ the best grades in the school.

10. We are in love. My girlfriend and I **_are engaged_** _____ each other.

11. The gorilla **_escaped_** _____ its cage and is now somewhere in the city.

12. The child **_was excited_** _____ going to the zoo.

13. The workers **_were exhausted_** _____ working in the sun all day.

Answers: (1) into; (2) in; (3) with; (4) with; (5) to; (6) on; (7) from ; (8) of or about (9) to; (10) to; (11) from; (12) about ; (13) from

Chapter 4 - Prepositions following verbs beginning with the letters **F**, **G**, **H**, and **I**

Using prepositions in expressions with certain verbs – beginning with the letters F, G, H, and I

Using prepositions in expressions with certain verbs - verbs beginning with the letters F, G, H and I

To be ***familiar with*** (something)

Examples:

- I ***am familiar with*** the laws in my country

  (meaning: I know what the laws are in my country).

To ***forgive*** (someone) ***for*** (something)

Examples:

- I ***forgive*** you ***for*** coming late.

- Rodney ***forgave*** the barber ***for*** the bad haircut.

To be ***fond of*** (something)

Examples:

- I ***am fond of*** Italian food. I eat it almost every night.

- Sarah *is* very *fond of* her boyfriend.

To be *friendly with / to* (someone)

Examples:

- The people of New Zealand *are* very *friendly to* foreigners.

- The woman who works at the pub *is* very *friendly with* the customers.

To be *frightened of* or *by* (something)

Examples:

- I *am frightened of* the dark.

- She *is frightened by* his behavior.

To be *full of* (something)

Examples:

- The car *is full of* gas.

- The arena *is full of* people.

To *get rid of* (something)

Examples:

- I am going to *get rid of* my old pants because they have too many holes in them.

- The company president wants to *get rid of* employees who are not working hard.

To be _**glad about**_ (somewhere)

Examples:

- Your team just won the game! Wow, I'_**m glad about**_ that.

- Kathy _**was glad about**_ finishing school.

To be _**good at**_ (something)

Examples:

- He'_**s good at**_ speaking English.

- Mr. Frankel _**is good at**_ teaching English.

To be _**good for**_ (something)

Examples:

- That hammer _**is good for**_ pounding nails into wood

- Yoga _**is good for**_ your health.

To be _**gone from**_ (somewhere)

Examples:

- I'll _**be gone from**_ the office for two hours.

- Hiromi _**was gone from**_ school for a week because of illness.

To _**graduate from**_ (somewhere)

Examples:

- She ***graduated from*** university last year with a degree in mathematics.

- John and I ***graduated from*** high school last year.

To ***happen to*** (do something)

Examples:

- When you were in school, did you ***happen to*** see your friend, Kazu? (***Happen to*** means 'by chance').

- When Joy was at the mall she ***happened to*** see her friend Alice.

To be ***happy about*** (something)

Examples:

- The student ***was*** very ***happy about*** getting an A on the exam.

- The shopkeeper ***was happy about*** all the customers that came to his store.

To ***hear about*** (something)

Examples:

- Did you ***hear about*** the bank robbery yesterday?

- We ***heard about*** the cancellation of the concert and we were not happy.

To ***hear from*** (someone)

Examples:

- She ***heard from*** her good friend in Japan. She got an email from her yesterday.

- I haven't ***heard from*** my brother in six months. I hope he's okay.

To ***help*** (someone) ***with*** (something)

Examples:

- I will ***help*** you ***with*** your homework.

- The clerk ***helped*** me ***with*** filling out the form.

To ***hide*** (something) ***from*** (someone)

Examples:

- He ***hid*** her birthday gift ***from*** her until the day of her birthday.

- The boy ***hid from*** his friend in order to surprise him when he arrived.

To ***hope for*** (something)

Examples:

- We ***are hoping for*** nice weather tomorrow because we want to have a picnic.

- The students who didn't study were ***hoping for*** an easy exam.

To ***insist on*** (something)

Examples:

- Because it was dark, the kind taxi driver **_insisted on_** walking us to our door.
- The young man **_insisted on_** driving the car before buying it.

To be **_interested in_** (something or someone)

Examples:

- The business student **_is interested in_** learning to speak English well.

- My sister and I **_are interested in_** investing in real estate.

To **_introduce_** (someone) **_to_** (someone)

Examples:

- I would like to **_introduce_** you **_to_** my friend, Stephan.

- Stefan **_introduced_** his friend **_to_** me.

To **_invite_** (someone) **_to_** (something)

Examples:

- I would like to **_invite_** you **_to_** my party.

- Shawn was **_invited to_** William's party.

To be **_involved in_** (something) **_with_** (someone)

Examples:

- We are working together to finish this school project; we ***are involved in*** this school project.

- The beautiful lady ***is involved with*** the prince of England. (Meaning: she is having a relationship with the prince.)

Let's practice and review:

Read the following sentences and fill in the blanks with the correct preposition. Answers can be found at the bottom of the page.

1. She'*s good* _____ English grammar.

2. My friend Bill is going to *get rid* ____ his old pants because they have too many holes in them.

3. Gene *is frightened* ____ lizards.

4. You just won the lottery! Wow, I am sure you *are glad* _____ that.

5. Brad *graduated* _____ English school last year and can now speak English very well.

6. The boss *will be gone* _____ the office for a day.

7. When you were shopping, did you *happen* _____ see your friend, Aiko?

8. Janet *was* very *happy* _____ getting a passing grade on the exam.

9. Did you **_hear_** _____ the terrible news yesterday?

10. The doorman **_insisted_** ____ carrying our luggage.

11. Jeff **_hid_** his girlfriend's birthday gift _____ her until the day of her graduation.

12. Claudia **_is interested_** ____ learning to speak English well.

13. The boss wants to **_invite_** you _____ the company party.

14. Four of us **_are involved_** ____ the community project.

15. I would like to **_introduce_** you ____ my friend, Frank.

16. He **_was familiar_** _____ the design of the engine.

Answers: (1) at; (2) of; (3) of; (4) about; (5) from; (6) from; (7) to; (8) about; (9) about (10) on; (11) from; (12) in; (13) to; (14) in; (15) to; (16) with

Chapter 5 - Prepositions following verbs
beginning with the letters **K**, **L**, and **M**

Using prepositions in expressions with certain verbs – beginning with the letters K, L, and M

To be _**kind to**_ (someone)

Examples:

- The young boy _**was**_ very _**kind to**_ the old lady and helped her to walk across the busy street.
- The clerk in the candy store _**was**_ always _**kind to**_ children. He gave them a free piece of candy when they came into the store.

To _**know about**_ (something)

Examples:

- The students didn't _**know about**_ the test that the teacher planned for next Tuesday.

- We were new students and didn't _**know about**_ the rules in the school.

To _**laugh at**_ (something or someone)

Examples:

- The people on the sidewalk _**laughed at**_ the funny car driving down the street.

- All the students *__laughed at__* him because he said something funny.

To *__listen to / for__* (someone or something)

Example:

- We *__listened to__* the rap music.

- We walked along the street late at night in the dark and we *__listened for__* any unusual noise.

  Meaning: we *__listened for__* something means that we were trying to hear something

To *__look at / for__* (something or someone)

Examples:

- We *__looked at__* the ocean for a hour.

- We were *__looking for__* the little girl. She was lost in the big department store.

To *__look forward to__* (something)

Examples:

- We are *__looking forward to__* going to Hawaii next month.

- Janice and Hiro were *__looking forward to__* the hiking trip.

To be *__mad at__* (someone)

Examples:

- My boss ***was mad at*** me because I didn't finish my work on time.

- The customer ***was mad at*** the bartender for giving him the wrong drink.

To be ***made of*** (something)

Examples:

- The house ***was made of*** wood.
- The jar ***was made of*** glass.

To be ***made for*** (someone)

Examples:

- The dress ***was made for*** that lady.

- These shoes ***were made*** especially ***for*** me.

To be ***married to*** (someone)

Examples:
- Ted ***is married to*** Alice.

- Darlene ***is married to*** Don.

To ***matter to*** (someone)

Examples:

- The project seemed small, but it ***mattered to*** the company.

    means: the project was important to the company even though it was a small project.

- Money doesn't ***matter to*** some people.

  means: money is not important to some people.

To be ***the matter with*** (someone or something)

Examples:

- I don't know what ***is the matter with*** this car, it won't start up!

  Means: The car has a problem and the motor won't start

- My brother was sick, but the doctors didn't know what ***was the matter with*** him.

To ***multiply*** (this) ***by*** (that)

Examples:

- If you ***multiply*** 10 ***by*** 10 the answer will be 100.

- ***Multiply*** 2 ***by*** 27 and the answer is 54.

To ***add*** (this) ***to*** / ***and*** (that)

Examples:

- If you ***add*** 10 ***to*** 10 the solution will be 20.

- ***Add*** 5 ***and*** 45 and the answer is 50.

To ***subtract*** (this) ***from*** (that)

Example:

- *__Subtract__* 10 *__from__* 15 and the answer is 5.
- If you *__subtract__* 100 *__from__* 1000 you get 900.

To *__divide__* (this) *__by__* (that)

Example:

- *__Divide__* 10 *__by__* 2 and the answer is 5.
- When 20 is *__divided__* *__by__* 2 the answer is 10.

Let's practice and review

Read and / or listen to the following sentences and fill in the blanks with the correct preposition. Answers can be found at the bottom of this page.

1. ***Subtract*** 15 _____ 30 and the answer is 15.

2. If you ***add*** 20 _____ 30 the solution will be 50.

3. What ***is the matter*** _____ this pen? It doesn't write!

4. Kaori ***is married*** _____ Kazu.

5. His wife ***was mad*** _____ him because he didn't take the garbage outside.

6. The building ***was made*** _____ stone.

7. The wedding dress ***was made*** ____ Yukiko.

8. If you ***multiply*** 5 ___ 5 the answer will be 25.

9. ***Divide*** 100 ___ 50 and the answer is 2.

10. The children are ***looking forward*** ____ going to the park tomorrow.

11. The people at the circus ***laughed*** ___ the funny clown.

12. We sat in the audience and ***listened*** _____ the orchestra.

Answers: (1) from; (2) and; (3) with; (4) to; (5) at (6) of; (7) for; (8) by *or* times; (9) by (10) to; (11) at; (12) to

Chapter 6 - Prepositions following verbs beginning with the letters <u>N</u>, <u>O</u>, <u>P</u>, and <u>Q</u>

Using prepositions in expressions with certain verbs – beginning with the letters N, O, P, and Q

To be ***nervous about*** (something)

Examples:

- The actress ***was nervous about*** going on stage.

- The students ***were nervous about*** the exam.

To be ***nice to*** (someone)

Examples:

- The owner of the store ***was nice to*** the children and gave them some candy bars.

- Chris ***is*** always ***nice to*** his cousins.

To be ***opposed to*** (something)

Examples:

- The people of that country ***were opposed to*** high taxes.

- The local people of the island ***were opposed to*** having visitors.

To *pay for* (something)

Examples:

- The clerk in the food store waited for the man to *pay for* the food.

- Please *pay for* your groceries at the checkout counter.

To be *patient with* (something or someone)

Examples:

- The teacher *was patient with* the new student.

- My sister didn't do well in school, but the teachers were patient with her.

To be *pleased with* / *about* (something or someone)

Examples:

- Tomoko *was pleased with* the new bracelet that she just bought.

- She *was* also *pleased about* getting such a good price.

To *point at* (something or someone)

Examples:

- The little girl *pointed at* the bird in the sky.

- It is not polite to *point at* someone.

To be ***polite to*** (someone)

Examples:

- Jim was very ***polite to*** the older woman.

- It is not ***polite to*** point at someone.

To be *prepared for* (something)

Examples:

- Students, please ***be prepared for*** the final exam next week.

- The people of the town ***were prepared for*** the big storm.

To *protect* (something / someone) *from* (something / someone)

Examples:

- The mother ***protected*** the child ***from*** the cold rain with an umbrella.

- The police ***protect*** us ***from*** crime.

To be *proud of* (someone or something)

Examples:

- Keoki was very ***proud of*** his daughter because she received good grades on her exams.

- We are ***proud of*** our soccer team.

To be _qualified for_ (something)

Examples:

- Eric **_was qualified for_** his new computer job. He had 4 years of training in the computer field.

- Joel was not **_qualified for_** the job he was doing.

Let's practice and review:

Read the following sentences and fill in the blanks with the correct preposition. Answers can be found below.

1. Jerry was very **_polite_** _____ the monks.

2. The teacher **_was patient_** _____ the beginning English students.

3. We **_paid_** _____ the food and left the restaurant.

4. Allison **_was pleased_** _____ the clothes she bought at the mall.

5. The guide **_pointed_** _____ the mountains in the east.

6. We **_weren't prepared_** _____ the big storm that came quickly.

7. The applicant **_wasn't qualified_** _____ the job he wanted.

8. My friend was very **_proud_** _____ his sister because she received good grades on her exams.

9. The business **_was nervous_** _____ making the investment.

10. The shop owner **_was nice_** _____ everyone who shopped there.

11. The president of the company _is opposed_ _____ hiring more employees.

Answers: (1) to; (2) with; (3) for; (4) with; (5) at; (6) for; (7) for; (8) of; (9) about (10) to; (11) to

Chapter 7 - Prepositions following verbs
beginning with the letters **R** and **S**

Using prepositions in expressions
with certain verbs – beginning with the letters
R and S

To be ***ready for*** (someone or something)

Examples:

- The doctor ***was ready for*** the next patient. We ***are ready for*** the long hike up the mountain. We have out boots and hiking equipment.

- When you are camping in the wild, you should be prepared for anything.

To be ***related to*** (someone or something)

Examples:

- Bob Moore ***is*** not ***related to*** Kathy Moore. They come from different families.

- This bad weather ***is*** not ***related to*** the storm that we heard about.

To ***rely on*** (someone or something)

Examples:

- The employee was never on time and could not do his job right. His boss could not **_rely on_** him (could not trust him) to do a good job.

- We **_relied on_** our tour guide to take us back to the hotel.

To be **_responsible for_** (someone / something)

Examples:

- Jim was the manager of his division in his company. He **_was responsible for_** his employees and their work.

- Peter **_is responsible for_** bringing the potato chips to the party.

To be **_sad about_** (something)

Examples:

- The little girl **_was sad about_** loosing her dog.

- Jennifer **_was sad about_** missing the bus.

To be **_safe from_** (something)

Examples:

- The family went into the storm shelter to **_be safe from_** the hurricane.

- Janet uses an anti-virus program on her computer to **_be safe from_** viruses.

To be **_satisfied with_** (someone /something)

Examples:

- Tomoko just bought a new car. She **_was_** very **_satisfied with_** the car. The car was just the right color and was easy to operate.

- Julie **_was satisfied with_** her grade on the exam.

To be **_scared of / by_** (someone / something)

Example:

- The people in the city **_were scared of_** the monster.

- The young children **_were scared by_** the loud noise on the street.

To **_search for_** (someone / something)

Examples:

- Jane could not find her car keys. She **_searched for_** them in her bedroom, living room and bathroom, but she could not find them.

- The police **_searched for_** the missing child.

To **_separate_** (someone / something) **_from_** (someone / something)

Examples:

- The woman bought some beautiful red flowers and green flowers. The florist put all of the flowers together in one bag. When the woman took the flowers home she **_separated_** the green flowers **_from_** the red flowers.

- The contest judges **_separate_** the good performances **_from_** the bad performances.

To be **_sick of_** (someone / something)

Examples:

- The student **_was sick of_** doing homework.

- Jack **_was sick of_** eating the same thing for lunch every day.

To be **_similar to_** (someone / something)

Examples:

- Janet went to the clothing shop to buy a dress. The clerk showed her a dress that **_was_** very **_similar to_** a dress that she already owned.

- This sports car **_is_** very **_similar to_** that one.

To be **_slow at_** (something)

Examples:

- The student **_was slow at_** learning math.

- In the beginning, the visitors **_were_** a little **_slow at_** understanding our culture.

To be **_surprised at / by_** (someone / something)

Examples:

- Hiroko **_was surprised at_** the store's high prices for food.

- Everyone **_was surprised at_** how expensive the dress was.

To **_be_** / **_feel sorry for_** (someone / something) **_about_** (something)

Examples:

- The family lost all of their possessions in the terrible storm. We **_feel_** very **_sorry for_** them.

- The boy broke the window with his soccer ball. He **_was_** very **_sorry for_** doing this.

- The thief **_was very sorry about_** stealing the little girl's money.

To **_speak to_** (someone) **_about_** (something)

Examples:

- Nicole **_spoke to_** Tom about the problem she was having at work.

- Maya **_spoke to_** her travel agent about her trip to Europe.

To **_stare at_** (someone / something)

Examples:

- Never **_stare at_** the sun.

- The two lovers **_stared at_** each other for a long time.

To be **_sure of_** (someone / something)

Examples:

- The student **_was sure of_** his answer. He wrote the answer on the test paper.

- Sandra was a confident person; she **_was sure of_** herself.

Let's practice and review

Read the following sentences and fill in the blanks with the correct preposition. Answers can be found on the bottom of the page.

1. Christine Smith **_is related_** ___ Allen Brock. They are brother and sister. Smith is Christine's married name.

2. You should not **_rely_** ____ other people to help you.

3. Stephan **_was responsible_** _____ maintenance of the company's cars.

4. Julie **_was sad_** _____ having to leave Hawaii after her vacation.

5. I went to my doctor and got a flu vaccine to **_be safe_** _____ the flu virus.

6. Allan's job at the factory is to **_separate_** the large parts _____ the small parts.

7. Annja **_searched_** _____ her car keys but could not find them.

8. The children at the zoo **_were scared_** _____ the lion.

9. Peter **_was satisfied_** _____ the car he just bought.

10. The operator **_was sick_** _____ hearing complaints from callers.

11. Jean **_was surprised_** _____ the number of people who came to her party.

12. We **_feel_** very **_sorry_** _____ people who lose family members.

13. The students **_were slow_** _____ learning the new lesson.

14. A girl came to the party wearing a dress that **_was_** very **_similar_** ___ the dress that Kyoko was wearing.

15. The team **_was sure_** _____ it's ability to win the soccer match.

16. Never **_stare_** _____ a stranger. It's impolite.

Answers: (1) to; (2) on; (3) for; (4) at; (5) from; (6) from; (7) for; (8) of; (9) with (10) of; (11) at; (12) for (13) at; (14) to; (15) of; (16) at

Chapter 8 - Prepositions following verbs beginning with the letters T through Z

Using prepositions in expressions with certain verbs – beginning with the letters T through Z

To **_take care of_** (someone / something)

Examples:

- The mother **_took care of_** the child.

- The businessman **_took care of_** the details needed to complete the business transaction.

To **_talk to / with_** (someone) **_about_** (something)

Examples:

- The boy's father **_talked to_** him about his poor grades in school.

- The new employee **_talked with_** some of her colleagues about her new job.

To **_tell_** (someone) **_about_** (someone / something)

Examples:

- The police **_told_** everyone **_about_** the prisoner that escaped.
- Mary told Christine about the new family who moved into the neighborhood.

To be **_terrible at_** (something)

Examples:

- Jack **_was terrible at_** math. He never got good grades on his math exams.

- When I was in high school, I **_was terrible at_** history.

To be **_terrified by_** / **_of_** (someone / something)

Examples:

- The little girl **_was terrified of_** the dark. She would never go outside of the house after dark.

- Jan's mother **_was terrified by_** snakes.

To **_thank_** (someone) **_for_** (something)

Example:

- The old lady **_thanked_** the boy **_for_** helping her to cross the street.

To be **_tired of_** (someone or something) (*similar to* **_sick of_**):

Example:

- The little boy **_was tired of_** eating vegetables at dinner time.

To be **_tired from_** (something)

Examples:

- The man **_was tired from_** working so hard.
- Andrew **_was tired from_** the workout.

To **_travel to_** (somewhere)

Examples:

- The girl and her boyfriend **_traveled to_** Las Vegas together.

- We plan on **_traveling to_** Indonesia this summer.

To be **_used to_** (something)

Examples:

- Jim walks to school every day. Walking to school was not a problem for Jim because he **_was used to_** doing it. (Same meaning as accustomed to)

- Megumi **_is used to_** spending many hours studying English.

To **_wait for_** (someone or something)

Examples:

- The people in the theater **_waited for_** the show to begin.

- We **_waited for_** the train for one hour.

To **_wait on_** (someone)

Examples:

- The waiter in the restaurant _**waited on**_ the customers.

- The stewardess _**waited on**_ the airline passengers.

To be _**worried about**_ (someone or something) (similar to _**worry about**_):

Examples:

- The mother _**was worried about**_ her sick child.

- Toby _**was worried about**_ his friend who was in the hospital.

Let's practice and review

Read the following sentences and fill in the blanks with the correct preposition. Answers can be found at the bottom of this chapter .

1. The nurse **_waited_** ____ her seriously ill patients.

2. The principal of the school **_was used_** ____ hearing the excuses of the late students.

3. We **_traveled_** _____ Honolulu last year.

4. The hikers **_were tired_** _____ walking so much.

5. The big, strong man **_was terrified_** _____ spiders.

6. The manager **_thanked_** his workers _____ their hard work.

7. The policeman **_talked_** ____ Jenny _____ her expired drivers license.

8. Fred **_was terrible_** _____ English grammar.

9. The lady next door **_told_** everyone _____ Mika's new boyfriend.

10. The baby sitter **_took care_** ____ the two children.

11. Everyone at the bus stop **_waited_** _____ the 12:05 bus.

12. The students **were worried** _____ the exam.

Answers: (1) on; (2) to; (3) to; (4) of; (5) of; (6) for; (7) to . . . about; (8) at; (9) about (10) of; (11) for; (12) about

Mastering English Prepositions

Section 3: Understanding the meanings and correct usage of all common English prepositions

Learn to use English prepositions correctly in all kinds of English sentences and conversation.

In this section, the student will find a comprehensive listing of the most commonly used prepositions in the English language, along with clear explanations about how to use them in different types of English sentences and plenty of examples to reinforce understanding.

Chapter 1 - English prepositions beginning with the letters <u>A</u> and <u>B</u>

This is a comprehensive listing of the most common English prepositions. The prepositions are followed by a usage explanation. After each explanation there are examples to help reinforce the correct use of the preposition in common English sentences.

Common English prepositions beginning with the letters A and B

Below we will explain these commonly used prepositions, give you many examples and give you some practice at the end of the chapters.

About

About: usually we use the word ***about*** before a topic or person

Examples:

- They are talking ***about*** the plan for next week.
- The newspaper story is ***about*** the bank robbery that took place last night.
- She is not talking ***about*** you she is talking about Betty.

About can also mean preparing to or getting ready to do something:

Example:

- She was ***about*** to leave when suddenly it began to rain.

Sometimes we use the word ***about*** to help describe a noun:

Example:

- There is something scary ***about*** that dark house.

Some **non**-prepositional uses for the word ***about:***

Examples:

- He did an ***about*** face (meaning: he changed his direction by 180 degrees).

- It's ***about*** time! You're late! We have been waiting for more than three hours.

Note: ***about*** can also be used as an adverb. The adverb ***about*** means almost:

Example:

- They are ***about*** done with the exam.

Above:

(the opposite of **above** is **below**)

Above: usually, ***above*** means higher than or over:

Examples

- Oh look at that bird flying ***above*** our heads.

- Look, this is very easy to understand. The ceiling is ***above*** us and the floor is beneath us. Got it?

- There are no subways in this city; all the trains travel ***above*** ground. (Our city has a good subway system; the trains travel ***below*** ground.)

Above: Sometimes ***above*** is used in a sentence to talk about a good person that has good values and judgment and would not do something wrong:

Example:

- The Buddhist monk is ***above*** stealing.
- A virtuous person is ***above*** hurting others.

Above: Sometimes ***above*** is used like in the above sentence but to mean that a person wrongly believes that they are better than, for example, the law.

Example:

- The politician thought that he was **_above_** the law. (meaning: the politician wrongly believed that he could commit crimes because he thought that he was higher than the law).

Above: Sometimes when you are reading something and it says to see something **_above_**. This means to look for something that was written before the section you are now reading.

Example:

- If you are having trouble using your new mp3 player, please see the **_above_** instructions.

Across

Across is usually used to talk about movement from one side to the other side of a space, area, or location:

Examples:

- The man walked **_across_** the street to visit his secret lover.

- The tiny boat sailed **_across_** the great Pacific Ocean.

- The satellite flew **_across_** the sky at great speed.

Across is often used to mean directly facing something or someone:

Example:

- The bank was directly **_across_** from the food store. (Meaning: *the bank's location and the food store's location were across from or facing each other)*

Across: Other uses for the preposition **_across_**:

Example:

- I came **_across_** a big sale while I was at the shopping mall. (Meaning: I discovered something I didn't expect to find while I was shopping.   Please see <u>Phrasal</u> <u>Verbs</u> for more information.)

After

(the opposite of **after** is **before**)

After is usually used to mean following or later than:

Examples:

- There was a big dinner **_after_** the wedding ceremony, and the bride and groom were toasted many times.

- Dessert came _**after**_ the main course, and it was delicious.
- I will be ready to go _**after**_ 9 a.m.; please don't rush me.
- _**After**_ breakfast, we went to the zoo and saw the new baby elephant.

**After** is used to mean something that happens continuously:

Example:

- The student studied night _**after**_ night for the final exam.

**After** is often used to mean to chase or to be in pursuit of:

Example:

- The soccer player ran _**after**_ the ball.

**After** can be used as a conjunction to connect two parts of a sentence:

Example:

- The teacher congratulated me _**after**_ I received a high mark.

Please see Gerunds and Infinitives for more information about gerunds that follow prepositions.

Against

Against can mean something forcibly hitting into or touching something else:

Example:

- He hit the tennis ball **_against_** the wall, but he didn't hit it very hard.

Against is usually used to mean to lean on or touch something or someone for support:

Example:

- You are such a lazy husband. The ladder is **_against_** the wall in the garage. Use this ladder to help to paint the house.

Against can mean in opposition to something:

Example:

- The people of the town were **_against_** higher taxes.

Against can also mean something that may not be an advantage; a disadvantage:

Example:

- They tried to repair the railroad tracks as quickly as possible, but time was **_against_** them; the next train would soon arrive.

Against: Other uses for the preposition **_against_** as in this English expression meaning 'impossible or unlikely':

Example:

- **_Against_** all odds, Hiro won the tournament.

Ahead of

Ahead of usually means to be located in front of:

Example:

- Kazu was ahead of Katrina in the lunch line. (Meaning, Katrina was closer to where lunch was being served than Kazu was.)

Ahead of can sometimes mean that someone or something is more advance than someone or something else:

Example:

- The student registered for classes one week late and so the other students were **_ahead of_** him.

Meaning: the other students had already been studying for one week. The new student was new to the class work.)

Along

Along usually means following the boundary of something:

Example:

- There were beautiful flowers (all) ***along*** the road.

Along can mean together:

Example:

- My friend Don decided to drive to Dallas, Texas. I decided to go ***along*** for the ride.

*Please refer to "Beyond Phrasal Verbs" book, for more information about the word **along**.*

Among

Among usually means surrounded by, included in a group, or many things or people in a group:

Examples:

- See, over there. You can see the house ***among*** the trees. There are ghosts in that house.

- The party was a lot of fun. I was ***among*** my friends so I felt very comfortable. We had a blast.

Around

Around can mean: follow a route (sometimes almost circular) to a desired location; located on the farther side of:

Example:

- The shopping center is ***around*** the corner from the bank, and two stores down from Wal-Mart. It's close to the park.

Around can mean following a boundary in a circular direction:

Examples:

- For excrcise we walk ***around*** the park, and then we do yoga and tai chi.
- The man traveled ***around*** the world by foot.

Around can mean walking or moving in many different directions randomly:

Example:

- We walked ***around*** the car show for about an hour and then we went home. We saw many interesting concept cars there.

*Please refer to the Focus on English book about "Beyond Phrasal Verbs" for more information about the word **around**.*

As

_As_ *can mean: in the role of:*

Example:

- Marco works **_as_** a mail clerk for the postal service.

*Please refer to the Focus on English book "Beyond Phrasal Verbs" for more information about the word **_as_**.*

At

_At_ is often used in expressing time:

Example:

- I have to be at the dentist office **_at_** 10 o'clock. Oh, I don't want to go!

_At_ is often used in talking about location:

Examples:

- He sat **_at_** his desk and sent emails to his girl friends.
- Example: There was someone **_at_** the door with a big package. I was so surprised.
- Example: We have to be **_at_** the show at 9 p.m., otherwise they will not allow us to enter the theater.

_At_ is used to express a level or rate:

Examples:

- The food store is selling tomatoes **_at_** $1.00 per pound. Boy, that's cheap!

- She is a good student. She is **_at_** the top of her class.

_At_ is sometimes used to express rate of speed:

Example:

- The policeman stopped Martin and told him that he was driving too fast. Martin was traveling **_at_** 75 miles per hour when the policeman saw him.

There are many uses for the word **at** after certain English verbs, in English phrasal verbs, and in English expressions (or idioms). Please refer to our "Beyond Phrasal Verbs" book.

Before

(the opposite of **before** is **after**)

Before is sometimes used in expressions of time, as in: earlier than a certain time:

Examples:

- The new student arrived in class **_before_** 9 a.m..

  - The bus usually arrives **_before_** 4 p.m..

  - Oh no, we have to be at school **_before_** 8 a.m. tomorrow morning because we have to prepare a presentation for the class. Oh, I can't get up that early!

Before is sometimes used to express order:

Examples:

- The B train comes **_before_** the J train. If you miss the B train you will have to wait for 1 hour for the next B train.

- The letter A comes **_before_** the letter B in the English alphabet.

Before is sometimes used to express the position of someone or something in relationship to something else:

Examples:

- The student was asked to stand **_before_** the class and give her presentation.

- The politician stood **_before_** the crowd and gave a speech.

Behind
(the opposite of **behind** is **ahead**)

Behind is sometimes used to express on the other side of something or someone; or to the rear of something:

Examples:

- The mouse is **_behind_** the wall, and it sounds like he's playing a clarinet.
- She hid her face **_behind_** her scarf because she was laughing at the boy who seemed so interested in her.

Behind is sometimes used in expressions of time, meaning late or not on schedule:

Example:

- We were supposed to finish the project yesterday, but we are **_behind_**.

Below
(the opposite of below is above)

Below is used to talk about rank, position or location in comparison to something or someone else:

Examples:

- We live in a valley **_below_** a big mountain. (location)
- The dish soap is in the cabinet **_below_** the sink. (location)
- The assistant director is **_below_** (lower in rank) the director. (rank)

Beneath
(similar in meaning to the preposition **underneath**)

Beneath means under something and sometimes hidden or concealed by something:

Examples:

- Your feet are ***beneath*** the desk. Do I need to tell you that?

- The rug is ***beneath*** your feet. Please take off your shoes because the rug is new.

Beneath can be used to mean that something or someone is less worthy than someone or something else:

Examples:

- I am well educated and have plenty of experience. That job is for people with no education or experience. That job is ***beneath*** me. I am better than that.

- How dare you accuse me of stealing! I come from a very good family with high virtues. Stealing is ***beneath*** me.

  (Meaning: I am too virtuous to commit a crime).

Beside
(similar in meaning to ***next to***)

Beside means very close by, next to:

Examples:

- My friend stood **_beside_** me while I applied for citizenship.

- Your bicycle is **_beside_** the house.

- The pencil is there, **_beside_** your book.

Beside can also be used to mean very upset, agitated or emotional:

Examples:

- The mother was **_beside_** herself when she heard that her daughter was in the hospital.

- The man who won the lottery was **_beside_** himself with joy.

Besides

Besides can mean _in addition to or apart from_; :

Examples:

- **_Besides_** being the best student in the school, she was also a good athlete.

  (meaning: **_in addition to_** being the best student . . .)

- You are not old enough to drink alcohol, and **_besides_** that, alcohol is not good for you.

(🕷 meaning: another reason why you shouldn't drink alcohol (**apart from** the fact that you are not old enough . . .)

Between

Between is used to talk about location of something, usually in the middle of two other things or people:

Examples:

- The grocery store is located ***between*** the bank and the library.

- I found my homework. It was ***between*** the first and second page of my grammar book.

Between is sometimes used in expressions of time: from (beginning with) one time to (ending with) another time :

Examples:

- We eat lunch ***between*** 12 p.m. and 1 p.m. every day.

- School is closed ***between*** June 1st, and August 1st.

Between is sometimes used to express sharing:

Examples:

- We went on our vacation with about $500 **between** us.

  (Meaning: together we had $500).

- The ice cream cone costs $1.75, but we only had $1.50 **between** us.

  (Meaning: together we only had $1.50, 75 cents each, not enough for the ice cream cone)

*There are other uses for the word **between** in English phrasal verbs and in English expressions (or idioms). Please refer to our book, "Beyond Phrasal Verbs".*

Beyond

Beyond is used to express that something's or someone's location is further ahead or on the other side of something / someone else :

Examples:

- Hello, I'm looking for the bank. Is it much further ahead?

  No, only a kilometer **beyond** the gas station.

- Excuse me, where is the restroom?

  The restroom is located just **beyond** the water fountain in that direction.

Beyond is sometimes used to express lack of understanding about something:

Examples:

- That math example was so hard. It was ***beyond*** me.
  (🔧 Meaning: the math example was beyond my understanding, or my ability to understand it).

- I heard that Keiko got a passing grade on the exam.

  How she ever passed that exam without studying is ***beyond*** me!

Beyond can also be used to express being ahead of something or someone:

Example:

- She is a very good English student; she is ***beyond*** me in grammar and writing.

  (🔧 Meaning: she is better than me at English grammar and writing)

By

By can be used in expression of time with the meaning not later than:

Examples:

- Why are you so worried?
  The teachers said that we have to have the homework done **_by_** Wednesday at 8am!

- Hurry, we have to be there **_by_** 5 p.m. or we will miss the show.

_By_ can be used to talk about a way or method of doing something:

Examples:

- You can calculate the solution to that problem **_by_** adding 5 and 8 together.

- I have to go to school **_by_** bus tomorrow because my car broke down.

- I went to Fiji **_by_** boat. Boy, that was a long trip!

_By_ can be used to can be used to mean near or next to:

Examples:

- My dog was sitting **_by_** my side.

- He parked his car **_by_** my car.

  (Meaning: he parked his car next to my car.)

_By_ can be used to express who or what caused something (usually used in passive sentences):

Examples:

- This house was built _**by**_ a carpenter.
- The building was destroyed _**by**_ the typhoon.
- The fingerprint marks on the wall were made _**by**_ the child.

_By_ can be used when talking about math, multiplication, division and expressing the measurements of rooms and geometric shapes:

Examples:

- The teacher told us that when we multiply 5 _**by**_ 6 the answer is 30.
- All four pieces of candy cost $1.00. To calculate how much each piece of candy costs, divide $1.00 _**by**_ 4. Each piece of candy costs 25 cents!
- The room measures 10 feet _**by**_ 50 feet. That's a big room!

*There are other uses for the word **by** in English phrasal verbs and in English expressions (or idioms). Please refer to our book, "Beyond Phrasal Verbs".*

Chapter Review
Prepositions beginning with the letters **A** and **B**

Instructions: read the sentences below. Decide whether the use of the preposition is correct or incorrect. If incorrect, which of these prepositions **best** fits the sentence: ***about, above, across, after, against, ahead of, along, among, around, as, at, before, behind, below, beneath, beside, besides, between, beyond, by***. The answers can be found at the bottom of this page.

1. Alfred is talking **about** the exam he took last night.
   □correct   □incorrect

2. The military planes are flying **beneath** our heads.
   □correct   □incorrect

3. The grocery store was directly **by** the street from the library.   □correct   □incorrect

4. The policeman ran **among** the criminal.   □correct
   □incorrect

5. The new bicycle is **against** the wall in the garage.
   □correct   □incorrect

6. Lila was **ahead** of Alicia and Tommy in the registration line.   □correct   □incorrect

7. There were many people **among** the road during the marathon.   □correct   □incorrect

8. Many people walk **around** the mall for exercise.
   ☐correct ☐incorrect

9. William works as a pizza maker for the pizza shop **on** the corner. ☐correct ☐incorrect

10. Mika sat **between** the table and read a book.
    ☐correct ☐incorrect

11. You are not late for work if you arrive **before** 9 a.m..
    ☐correct ☐incorrect

12. The vice president is **about** the president in rank.
    ☐correct ☐incorrect

13. The new floor tile is **beneath** my feet. ☐correct ☐incorrect

14. Your bicycle is **above** the house. ☐correct ☐incorrect

15. You can find the bank **between** the pet store and the fire station. ☐correct ☐incorrect

16. The grocery store is located just **along** the water fountain. ☐correct ☐incorrect

Answers: (1) correct; (2) incorrect; should be <u>above</u>; (3) incorrect; should be <u>across</u>; (4) incorrect; should be <u>after</u>; (5) correct; (6) correct; (7) incorrect; should be <u>along</u>; (8) correct; (9) correct (10) incorrect; should be <u>at</u>; (11)

correct; (12) incorrect; should be **above** (13) correct; (14) incorrect; should be **by** *or* **beside**; (15) correct; (16) incorrect; should be **beside**

Chapter 2 - English prepositions beginning with the letters <u>C</u> - <u>F</u>

This is a comprehensive listing of the most common English prepositions beginning with the letters **C** through **F**. The prepositions are followed by a usage explanation. After each explanation there are examples to help reinforce the correct use of the preposition in common English sentences.

Common English prepositions beginning with the letters C - F

Below we will discuss the commonly used prepositions beginning with the letters **C** through **F**.

Close to

Close to is used to express nearness or nearly (almost):

Examples:

- Where is the shopping mall?
  The shopping mall is ***close to*** the park.

- I am very ***close to*** my family.

- I received ***close to*** 100 emails this morning (meaning, almost 100 emails)! I'm tired of spam!

Despite

Despite (In Spite Of) is used with a similar meaning to even though or notwithstanding:

Examples:

- **_Despite_** the rain, we will still have a picnic.
- He did well on the exam **_despite_** the difficult questions.
- He can kick a soccer ball hard **_despite_** the fact that he has weak legs.

Down

Down is used with a similar meaning to along when talking about travel:

Examples:

- We walked **_down_** the road for about 2 miles and then stopped at the lake.
- My friend drove **_down_** the highway at about 100 miles per hour. I was really scared!

Down is used to talk about going from a higher place to a lower place:

Examples:

- The divers went **_down_** to the bottom of the lake.

- He was playing cards with his friends and he was loosing money. He threw the cards ***down*** on the table in anger.

*There are other uses for the word **down** in English phrasal verbs and in English expressions (or idioms). Please refer to our book, "Beyond Phrasal Verbs".*

During

During is used in expressions of time; meaning within a period of time or meaning at the same time as something else is happening:

Examples:

- I wrote my friend an email ***during*** the morning break. (within a period of time)
- I got up ***during*** the show and bought my girlfriend some popcorn. (at the same time as the show was occurring)

Far From

Far From is used to talk about distance with the meaning that something is located a long way apart from something else:

Examples:

- The airport was ***far from*** the city center.

- Everyone moved *far* away *from* the entrance so that other people could enter the room easily.

For

For: Use *for* in conversation to indicate a special purpose for something or someone:

Examples:

- He uses a motorcycle *for* transportation.
- She wears that outfit *for* the beach.
- Do you give a gift to your girlfriend when she gets a good grade on her exams? No, I usually don't give gifts *for* that reason.
- My friend gave me a gift *for* Christmas.
- We wore costumes *for* Halloween.

For: Use *for* in conversation to talk about time (usually length of time or to indicate future time):

Examples:

- I have been in New York *for* 3 months. (length of time)
- I have been studying English *for* 2 years. (length of time)
- I am studying now *for* the test next week. (future time)

For: Use *for* to express who or what is the recipient:

Examples:

- They played the song *for* him.
- My wife has a gift *for* me.
- The engineer has some information *for* his boss.
- I bought gas *for* the car.

For: Use *for* to explain the reason or benefit of doing something:

Examples:

- The student apologized *for* getting a bad grade. (reason)
- The woman was paid *for* cleaning the house. (reason)
- The boy was scolded *for* stealing the apple. (reason)
- We go surfing *for* fun. (benefit)
- We speak English to everyone *for* practice. (benefit)

For: Use *for* to talk about financial transactions:

Examples:

- Apples are $5 *for* 3 pounds.

- After he repaired the woman's car, he handed her a bill *for* $1,000!
- How much does he get paid?
  He works *for* $10 an hour.

For: Use *for* to express an unusual talent or sense:

Examples:

- Marco can sing any song just by listening to it! He has an ear *for* music.
- That woman has an eye for good art. She buys and sells art *for* an art gallery.

For: Use *for* to express an unusual fact:

Examples:

- That woman has big feet *for* such a small person.
- Boy, it's really cold *for* July!

*There are other uses for the word *for* in English phrasal verbs and in English expressions (or idioms). Please refer to our book, "Beyond Phrasal Verbs".*

From
(the opposite of *from* is *to*)

From can be used in expressions of time:

Examples:

- The advanced English course runs **_from_** April 1st through April 30th. (**_From_**, in this example, has the meaning of 'beginning on.')

- The celebration runs **_from_** 5 p.m. on.
  (Meaning: **_From_** 5 p.m. until an unknown time in the future)

- We will see the exhibit one month **_from_** today.
  (Meaning: one month's time, beginning today)

From can be used to indicate where something came from, source:

Examples:

- I got a letter **_from_** my friend in China.

- Peaches come **_from_** Georgia.

- The brother and sister get money **_from_** their parents.

- He doesn't come **_from_** Europe. He comes **_from_** South Africa.

From can be used to indicate source + separation:

Examples:

- She borrowed money _**from**_ her friend. (The friend was the source and money was separated _**from**_ her and was lent to her friend).
- The scientists tried to protect the whales _**from**_ harm. (Separating the whales from harm)

**From** can be used to indicate distance (and separation) away:

Examples:

- My aunt lives 25 miles _**from**_ here.
- New York City is 2,905 miles _**from**_ San Francisco.
- The racing cars raced passed us and then disappeared _**from**_ view very quickly.

**From** is used in discussing math, especially subtraction:

Examples:

- Two _**from**_ four equals two.
- 100 _**from**_ 1000 = 900

**From** can answer the question why; _**from**_ can mean because of:

Examples:

- Why are they tired? They are tired _**from**_ running all day.

- Why are they so overweight? They are overweight _**from**_ eating too much.

From can be used to talk about what something is made of:

Examples:

- The sweater was made _**from**_ wool.
- The shoes were made _**from**_ leather.
- The apple tree was grown _**from**_ a seed.

From can be used to talk about position in relation to something or someone else (usually referring to viewing or listening):

Examples:

- We can see the fireworks _**from**_ our window.
- I could hear the speech _**from**_ the back of the room.

There are other uses for the word **from** in English phrasal verbs and in English expressions (or idioms). Please refer to our book, "Beyond Phrasal Verbs".

Chapter 2 <u>review</u>

*Prepositions beginning with the letters **C** through **F**
Instructions: read and / or listen carefully to the
sentences below. Decide whether the use of the
preposition is correct or incorrect. If incorrect, which of
these prepositions **best** fits the sentence: **close to**, **despite**,
down, **during**, **far from**, **for**, **from**. The answers can be
found at the bottom of this page.*

1. Go **down** the road for about 3 miles, and then turn
    left at the red light. ☐correct   ☐incorrect

2. A student raised his hand **close to** the class and
    asked a question. ☐correct   ☐incorrect

3. The library is **far from** the school building.
    ☐correct   ☐incorrect

4. The workers use the machine **except** digging the
    earth. ☐correct   ☐incorrect

5. Jean received an email **close to** her friend in
    Spain. ☐correct   ☐incorrect

6. The members of the soccer team are tired **from**
    the workout. ☐correct   ☐incorrect

7. **Despite** the bad weather, our team won the match.
    ☐correct   ☐incorrect

8. I went for a swim **during** the afternoon. ☐correct
☐incorrect

9. Alex borrowed money **down** Tricia. ☐correct
☐incorrect

10. The company sells products **for** a profit. ☐correct
☐incorrect

Answers: (1) correct; (2) incorrect; should be during; (3) correct; (4) incorrect; should be for; (5) incorrect; should be from; (6) correct; (7) correct; (8) correct; (9) incorrect; should be from; (10) correct

Chapter 3 - English prepositions beginning with the letters I̲ - N̲

This is a comprehensive listing of the most common English prepositions beginning with the letters *I̲* - *N̲*. The prepositions are followed by a usage explanation. After each explanation there are examples to help reinforce the correct use of the preposition in common English sentences.

Common English prepositions beginning with the letters I - N

Below wc will discuss these commonly used prepositions and provide you with many examples.

In

In is used to talk about a person's or thing's location inside of something:

Examples:

- She was sitting ***in*** the room.
- He was watching television ***in*** his house.
- The pen was ***in*** the drawer.

In is used to talk about a location direction:

Examples:

- The sun sets *in* the west.
- Beautiful woven rugs are made *in* the east.

In is used to talk about being inside of a location boundary, city, country, state, etc:

Examples:

- Right now, we are *in* New York City.
- My friend lives *in* San Francisco.
- Tokyo is *in* Japan.
- We are *in* the park.

    (What is the difference between *at* the park and *in* the park? We say that we are *in* the park when we are within the boundaries of the park. We often say we are *at* the park when we have arrived near to the park boundary. Sometimes, English speakers use *in* and *at* interchangeably when referring to locations like airport, library, school, park, etc. Example: Where are you now? I'm *at* the park; or, I'm *in* the park. Generally, *at* refers to being located close to or on the border of a location, whereas *in* refers to being inside the boundaries of the location.)

In is used to talk about time:

Examples:

- He was born in Okinawa, *in* 1983.
- I'm late! I have to be at school *in* 10 minutes!

- My wife should be home *in* 2 hours.
- We usually start school *in* September.
- My mother will be arriving *in* two weeks.
- They take their shower *in* the morning.
- We watch the sun set *in* the evening.
- I think we were happier *in* the 1970s. (or: *in* the 70s)

In: Use *in* when talking about weather:

Examples:

- We like to walk *in* the rain.
- It's hot *in* the sun.

In: Use *in* when talking about what someone is wearing:

Examples:

- She went to dinner *in* a beautiful black dress.
- They went to the Halloween party *in* a funny costume.

In: Use *in* when talking about a location on the body:

Examples:

- He was hit *in* the chest.
- She put her contact lens *in* her eye.

- The soccer player has a pain _**in**_ his foot.

_**In**_: Use _**in**_ when talking about how people relate to each other:

Examples:

- They were _**in**_ an argument last night.
- All of the members of the group worked _**in**_ cooperation with each other to solve the problem.
- The mother asked the little boy why his shirt was torn.
  The little boy told his mother that he was _**in**_ a fight.

_**In**_: Use _**in**_ when talking about the current status of something or someone:

Examples:

- The old book is still very popular. It is still _**in**_ print.
- That recipe is very famous and is _**in**_ demand.
  (☞ Meaning: many people would like to have it)

_**In**_: Use _**in**_ when you want to be clear about measurement:

Examples:

- He is very heavy. I don't know what he weighs *in* kilos, but *in* pounds he weighs more than 300.
- The car is very tall *in* height.

There are many other uses for the word in in English phrasal verbs and in English expressions (or idioms). To learn more, please refer to our book, "Beyond Phrasal Verbs".

In Back of

In Back of means to the rear of or behind:

Examples:

- They keep the garbage cans *in back of* the building.
- The garage is *in back of* the house.

In Front of

In Front of refers to something or someone that is located before or facing something or someone:

Examples:

- The woman stood *in front of* the mirror combing her hair.

- The car was parked *in front of* the school building.

Inside

Inside refers to something or someone that is located within something else:

Examples:

- The pencils are *inside* that red box.
- The two girls are *inside* that house.

Instead of

Instead of means to substitute something for something else:

Examples:

- We went swimming *instead of* surfing.
- Kazu studied English *instead of* Italian.

Into

Into is used to mean enter:

Examples:

- The businessman stepped *into* the cab.
- The English student went *into* the classroom.

- The flower shop girl put the flowers ***into*** a bag.

Into is sometimes used to mean something of interest or an occupation or preoccupation:

Examples:

- The students are really ***into*** learning English. (The students really enjoy learning English.)
- He loves soccer; he is really ***into*** soccer!

Into is sometimes used to talk about math division:

Examples:

- 12 ***into*** 48 equals 4.
- Ten ***into*** one hundred equals ten.

Into is used to talk about a condition change:

Examples:

- The student got ***into*** trouble for cheating on the exam.
- Kyoko got ***into*** debt after buying the expensive home.

Into is used to talk about sudden, hard contact, or forced contact with something or someone:

Examples:

- The motorcycle crashed ***into*** the building but the driver was not seriously hurt.

- The girl ran ***into*** the tree and had to be taken to the hospital.

*There are many other uses for the word **into** in English phrasal verbs and in English expressions (or idioms). Please see our book, "Beyond Phrasal Verbs".*

Like

Like is used to talk about similarities:

Examples:

- There is no other person ***like*** him.

- Places ***like*** New York and Los Angeles can be interesting vacation stops.

- He is ***like*** his brother. They both enjoy playing sports.

Like is used to talk about examples:

Examples:

- There are many forms of transportation, ***like*** cars, trains and planes.

- There are many things you can do to improve your English, ***like*** talking to native speakers, studying grammar, and attending classes regularly.

Near

Near is used to talk about distance from or location; something that is close by:

Examples:

- Oh, look at the tall buildings, we must be **_near_** Dallas.

- The whiteboard is **_near_** the door.

Next to

Next to is used to talk about something or someone that is near, close to, or in very close proximity to

Examples:

- She parked her car **_next to_** mine in the mall parking lot.

- Could you tell me where the grocery store is? Yes, it is **_next to_** the bank on Smith Street.

Chapter 3 <u>review</u>

*Prepositions beginning with the letters **I** - **N***

*Instructions: read the sentences below. Decide whether the use of the underlined preposition is correct or incorrect. If incorrect, which of these prepositions **best** fits the sentence: **in, in back of, in front of, inside, instead of, into, like, near, next**. The answers can be found at the end of the practice.*

1. I waited <u>in near of</u> the taxi stand for two hours, but no taxi came. □correct □incorrect

2. The car is <u>inside</u> the garage. □correct □incorrect

3. The businessman went <u>into</u> the building. □correct □incorrect

4. Places <u>like</u> Honolulu and Cancun can be nice for vacations. □correct □incorrect

5. Long Island is a place <u>instead of</u> New York City. □correct □incorrect

6. The bus stopped <u>next to</u> the shopping center. □correct □incorrect

7. One hundred <u>near</u> one thousand equals ten. □correct □incorrect

8. We went swimming <u>instead</u> <u>of</u> surfing. ☐correct ☐incorrect

9. Jim and Nancy got <u>into</u> debt when they bought the expensive sports car. ☐correct ☐incorrect

10. The garbage bins are <u>in</u> <u>back</u> <u>of</u> the store . ☐correct ☐incorrect

Answers: (1) incorrect; should be <u>in front of</u>; (2) correct; (3) correct; (4) correct; (5) incorrect; should be <u>near;</u> (6) correct; (7) incorrect; should be <u>into;</u> (8) correct; (9) correct; (10) correct

Chapter 4 - English prepositions beginning with the letter <u>O</u>

This is a comprehensive listing of the most common English prepositions beginning with the letter <u>*O*</u>. The prepositions are followed by a usage explanation. After each explanation there are examples to help reinforce the correct use of the preposition in common English sentences.

Common English prepositions beginning with the letter O

Below we will discuss these commonly used prepositions and provide you with many examples.

Of

<u>***Of***</u> is used to talk about belonging to or being connected to a group, something, someone or time:

Examples:

- Who is that tall man there?
  He is the dean <u>***of***</u> this college.

- That monk is <u>***of***</u> the Buddhist religion.

- That man is a citizen <u>***of***</u> the USA.

- Who is she?
  She is a doctor *of* medicine.
- The author is writing a book on the trees and plants *of* Australia.
- We watched fireworks on the fourth *of* July.
- April Fools day is on the first day *of* April.
- I finished my English studies in March *of* last year.

Of is used to help talk about categories or types of things or people:

Examples:

- He was very embarrassed; the color *of* his face was red.
- The cost *of* the home was very high.
- Before you can order shoes, you have to know the size *of* your foot.
- I don't like the smell *of* that fish. I think it is bad.
- My mother bought two bags *of* rice yesterday.

Of is used to help talk about quantity:

Examples:

- Are we going to be late?
  No, we have plenty *of* time.

- Many *of* the people who listen to EnglishMP3 audio books learn English well.

- We have hundreds *of* products in our store.

- Don't worry about breaking the dish; we have plenty *of* dishes.

There are many other uses for the word of in English phrasal verbs and in English expressions (or idioms). Please refer to our book, "Beyond Phrasal Verbs".

Off

Off is used to talk about a condition or state of being; that something is not on or has stopped functioning:

Examples:
- The stove is cool. It must be *off*.

- Would you please turn *off* all the lights? Electricity is expensive.

- Well, that show was terrible. I think I will turn *off* the TV now.

- Did we turn the stove *off* before we left home? Yes, remember? I turned it *off* 10 minutes before we left the house.

Off is used to talk about movement that represents change in location:

Examples:

- The papers blew *off* the table.
- The motorcycle ran *off* the road but the driver was not hurt.

Off can be used to mean to remove or separate:

Examples:
- Mary, did you take your books *off* the counter? Yes mom, my books are *off* the counter.
- My father shaved *off* his beard. Boy, his appearance really changed!

Off can be used to mean to stop doing something:

Examples:
- Do you want to go to the club with me? I can't because I'm *off* alcohol.

  (Meaning: I don't want to drink alcohol any more.)
- What time do you get *off* work?

  (Meaning: What time do you stop work.) I get *off* at 4 p.m..

Off is used to mean not far from:

Examples:

- The bank is just **_off_** Elm Street.

  (Meaning: A little bit further past or in the vicinity of Elm Street.)

- Oh, that was a terrible golf shot. You're a little **_off_** today. (Meaning: You are not playing like you usually do; your golf game is not as good as usual.)

Off is sometimes used in commands and warning signs to mean do not have contact with:

Examples:

- Please keep **_off_** the grass!
- Wet concrete, keep **_off_**!

*There are many other uses for the word **off** in English phrasal verbs and in English expressions (or idioms). Please see our book "Beyond Phrasal Verbs".*

On

_On_ can mean contact with a surface or surface location:

Examples:

- The books are **_on_** the desk.
- The picture is **_on_** the wall.
- The fly is **_on_** the window.
- The writing is **_on_** the wall.

- The woman is driving her car **_on_** the street.
- The boy is riding his skateboard **_on_** the sidewalk.

_On_ can mean in contact but above something else:

Examples:

- Please print your name **_on_** the line.

_On_ can mean a location, usually outdoors:

Examples:

- The parking garage is **_on_** the side of the building.
- Where are you?
  We're **_on_** the corner of Elm and Second Avenue.
- We went **_on_** the roof to get the cat.
- We all live **_on_** the planet called Earth.

_On_ is used to talk about time:

Examples:

- I have to go to the doctor's office **_on_** Wednesday.
- My family is coming to visit **_on_** Christmas day.
- We will arrive **_on_** Monday.

On is used when talking about transportation and traveling:

Examples:

- They got ***on*** the bus.
- She was ***on*** the train for two hours.
- The family spent four hours ***on*** the plane.

(Note: use ***in*** when talking about a taxi or car. Example: The businessman was ***in*** the taxi for an hour because of heavy traffic.)

On is used to talk about membership or being part of *something:*

Examples:

- My name is ***on*** the good student list.
- He is ***on*** the soccer team.

On is used to talk about means or resource:

Examples:

- The space shuttle rocket runs ***on*** special fuel.
- My wife and I live ***on*** my paycheck.
- The three mountain climbers survived ***on*** little water.

On can sometimes indicate the cause of a mishap or problem:

Examples:

- The boy hurt himself **_on_** his skateboard.
- She got sick **_on_** the bad food she ate at the restaurant.

On can sometimes indicate a reason for doing something:

Examples:

- They went to Fiji **_on_** vacation.
- Michael went to New York **_on_** business.

_On_ is sometimes used to indicate subject or topic; meaning about:

Examples:

- I read an article **_on_** how to learn English quickly.
- Their class presentation was **_on_** the environment.

_On_ can be used to indicate possession:

Examples:

- Can I borrow $5?
  Sorry, I don't have any money **_on_** me.
- Excuse me. Do you have a pen **_on_** you? I need to write down a phone number.

_On_ is used to indicate a special occasion:

Examples:

- Congratulations **_on_** getting married.
- They celebrated by going out dancing **_on_** their anniversary.

_On_ can indicate status, condition, or state:

Examples:

- Your new shoes are **_on_** order and should arrive next week.
- The woman is **_on_** a diet. She is trying to lose 30 pounds.

_On_ can be used to indicate a continuation of what was being done:

Examples:

- After stopping at the motel, we drove **_on_** to our next destination.
- We stopped to look at the accident, but the police told us to move **_on_**.

_On_ is used to talk about how something was communicated:

Examples:

- I learned about the new job opportunity **_on_** the Internet.
- I saw the advertisement **_on_** TV.

- Stefan and his brother heard the news **_on_** the radio.

_On_ is used to talk about behavior towards something or someone:

Examples:

- The long days without food or water were hard **_on_** the survivors. It was the biggest challenge of their lives.

- The test was too easy **_on_** the students. Everyone got a very high mark!

_On_ can help to express adding to something or acquiring something:

Examples:

- Jim wants to add **_on_** a bedroom to his house.

- The school added **_on_** five new teachers.

_On_ can be used to express two things happening at the same time (in this usage, on and upon can be used interchangeably):

Examples:

- **_On_** second thought, he decided not to buy the car.

- He called the fire department **_on_** seeing the fire in the house.

_On_ can be used to help express feelings or attitude towards something or someone:

Examples:

- The girl in the second row has a crush **_on_** the boy in the front of the class. (Meaning: she has a romantic interest in him.)

- The man took pity **_on_** the homeless man and gave him some money.

There are many other uses for the word **on** in English phrasal verbs and in English expressions (or idioms). Please see our book "Beyond Phrasal Verbs".

Onto

Onto _is used to talk about moving from one place to another place:_

Examples:

- The spider jumped **_onto_** the table.

- It was raining so they moved all of the picnic food **_onto_** a table that was under an umbrella.

Opposite

Opposite is used to mean across from:

Examples:

- Excuse me. Could you tell me where the bank is located?
  Yes. The bank is up that street ***opposite*** the grocery store.
- She sat ***opposite*** her boyfriend at the fancy restaurant.

Out

Out is used when talking about passing something around or distributing something:

Examples:

- Sally, would you please pass ***out*** these forms to the class.

- We mailed ***out*** about 1,000 brochures to advertise our new business.

Out is used when talking about removing something or someone:

Examples:

- I brought the gift ***out*** to the car. I'm bringing it to my sister's birthday party.

- She opened the box and took ***out*** the new dress.

*****Out*** is often used with the preposition of in expressing different ideas in English. Below are some usage explanations and examples for **out of**.*

Out _of_ can be used to express absence:

Examples:

- Three **_out_** of five people today do not exercise regularly.

- Two **_out_** of every three of these apples are bad. We should take this bag of apples back to the market.

Out _of_ can be used to express a percentage or fraction of something:

Examples:

- Hello Marta. I haven't seen your sister in a week. Where is she?
  Oh, she is **_out_ _of_** the country. She will be back next week.

- Mr. Yoshida is **_out_ _of_** the office at the moment, may I take a message for him?

- Hello? No, Gerhard is not here right now. He is **_out_ _of_** town.

Out _of_ can be used to express not being normal or not what is usually expected:

Examples:

- Oh my gosh, that coat is so **_out_ _of_** style!

- What happened?

  That car went **_out_ _of_** control and hit the telephone pole!

Out _of_ can be used to express what something was made of or what ingredients went into making something:

Examples:

- That company makes surfboards **_out_ _of_** bamboo.

- Cotton candy is made **_out_ _of_** pure sugar.

Out _of_ can be used to express a lack of or no longer available or in supply:

Examples:

- I drove to the gas station to get some fuel for my car, but the gas station was **_out_ _of_** fuel.

- I would like to have a vanilla ice cream cone, please.
  Sorry. We are all **_out_ _of_** vanilla.

  (Note: the word **_all_** used with **_out_ _of_** means **_completely_**.)

Out _of_ can mean away from, similar to distance from:

Examples:

- Excuse me. Could you tell me where the nearest gas station is?
  Yes. It's on this road about four miles **_out_ _of_** town.

- If you want to buy alcohol, you will have to go ***out of*** state because it is illegal in this state to sell alcohol.

Out of can be used to express a reason for doing something:

Examples:

- I went to Bali ***out of*** curiosity. I've always wanted to see what that island was like.

- I adopted the stray cat ***out of*** pity.

*There are many other uses for the word **out** in English phrasal verbs and in English expressions (or idioms). Please see our book, "Beyoind Phrasal Verbs".*

Outside

Outside is often used with the preposition *of*. Outside means not within the confines of something:

Examples:

- We could hear strange noises ***outside*** the house.

- The man put his wet boots ***outside*** the door.

Over

Over means above something or someone; it usually indicates being higher than:

Examples:

- We flew **_over_** New York on our way to Boston.

- The branch of the tree hung **_over_** the house.

- The price of that car is expensive. It's way **_over_** my head because I don't earn that much money.

- I don't understand Einstein. His theories are way **_over_** my head.

   (Meaning: I can't understand his theories because they are too complicated for me.)

Over is used to mean to cover something or someone:

Examples:

- The workers put a steel plate **_over_** the hole in the road.

- It was cold in the room so she put a sweater on **_over_** her blouse.

Over is used to express above and then to the other side of something or someone:

Examples:

- The runner jumped _**over**_ the branch that was in the road.
- The football player kicked the ball _**over**_ the wall.
- We had to climb _**over**_ the fence to get into the park.
- Is it possible to jump _**over**_ a rainbow?
- You should drive your car slowly _**over**_ a speed bump.

**Over** is used to express control over something or someone:

Examples:

- The emperor rules _**over**_ the people in his country.
- The general manager of the company is _**over**_ all employees.

**Over** is used to express location away from and on the other side of something or someone else:

Examples:

- The market is _**over**_ there.
- I work in a building that is just _**over**_ the bridge.

  (Note: the word **_just_** is used to mean **_a small distance from_**.)

Over can be used to indicate topic or subject:

Examples:

- We fought *over* who should pay the check at the restaurant.
- The leader of the country worried *over* the shortage of food.

Over (adverb) can mean finished:

Examples:

- The show is *over*.
- School is *over*.

*There are many other uses for the word **over** in English phrasal verbs and in English expressions (or idioms). Please see our book, "Beyond Phrasal Verbs".*

Chapter 4 review
*Prepositions beginning with the letter **O***

*Instructions: read the sentences below. Decide whether the use of the preposition is correct or incorrect. If incorrect, which of these prepositions **best** fits the sentence: **of**, **off**, **on**, **onto**, **on top of**, **opposite**, **out**, **outside**, **over**. The answers can be found at the bottom of this page.*

1. The priest is <u>of</u> the Catholic faith. ☐correct ☐incorrect

2. The final semester ends in June <u>on top of</u> this year. ☐correct ☐incorrect

3. My friend shaved the hair <u>off</u> his head. ☐correct ☐incorrect

4. The butter is <u>on</u> the table. ☐correct ☐incorrect

5. She was <u>out</u> the train for two hours. ☐correct ☐incorrect

6. The dancer jumped <u>onto</u> the stage. ☐correct ☐incorrect

7. The two buildings are <u>opposite</u> each other. ☐correct ☐incorrect

8. The student turned <u>of</u> the lights in the classroom. ☐correct ☐incorrect

9. Jonathan is <u>out</u> <u>of</u> the country. ☐correct
   ☐incorrect

10. The two girls fought <u>over</u> the good-looking boy.
    ☐correct   ☐incorrect

Answers: (1) correct; (2) incorrect; should be <u>of</u>; (3) correct; (4) correct; (5) incorrect; should be <u>on;</u> (6) correct; (7) correct; (8) incorrect; should be <u>off</u>; (9) correct; (10) correct

Chapter 5 - English prepositions beginning with the letters P - T

This is a comprehensive listing of the most common English prepositions beginning with the letters *P* - *T*. The prepositions are followed by a usage explanation. After each explanation there are examples to help reinforce the correct use of the preposition in common English sentences.

Common English prepositions beginning with the letters P - T

Below we will discuss these commonly used prepositions and provide you with many examples.

Past

Past is used to mean beyond:

Examples:

- Excuse me. How do I get to the theater. Just go up this street *past* the stop light and the theater is on your left.

- The director's office is just *past* classroom number 3 on the right side of the hall.

Past can mean to go by something or someone:

Examples:

- The girl walks *__past__* the pastry shop on her way to school every day.

- We drove *__past__* Lincoln Center in New York City.

Since

__Since__ means continuously or intermittently from a time in the past until the present:

Examples:

- I haven't been in Tokyo *__since__* last September.

- The school has been open *__since__* 1995.

- He hasn't said hello *__since__* we had that argument.

Through

__Through__ can be used to express passage, or movement, across or under a potential barrier or obstacle:

Examples:

- The five limousines passed *__through__* the open gate.

- I got a ticket for going *__through__* a red light.

- As we walked ***through*** the door, our whole family was there to greet us.

- We drove ***through*** the tunnel without our lights on. Boy, it was dark in there.

Through can be used to mean contiguous or sequential

(🖐️Meaning: one thing occurring in exact order after the other) with a beginning and an ending:

Examples:

- The students were asked to read pages 24 ***through*** 31 for their homework.

- My dad works Monday ***through*** Friday at the factory.

- The sale will continue on ***through*** Tuesday of next week.

Through can be used to express passage or movement within a confining space or borders:

Examples:

- We passed ***through*** the long, dark hallway as we walked to the waiting room.

- We walked ***through*** the park on our way home.

Through can relate to vision; being able to see something beyond the initial surface:

Examples:

- We looked ***through*** the window and saw the city below.

- My car needs new paint. I can see the metal showing ***through*** the paint in some spots.

Through is used to express completing something that may require hard work to finish:

Examples:

- I want to travel a lot, but first I have to get ***through*** school.

- That was a bad storm. I didn't think we were going to get ***through*** it.

- She went ***through*** a bad experience, but now she feels better.

Through is used with the word all to have the same meaning as throughout (Meaning: in all parts, or during an entire event):

Examples:

- My girlfriend and I walked all ***through*** the park looking at the gardens and enjoying the sunshine.

- That cat was crying all ***through*** the night. I hardly got any sleep!

Through is used to express the reason for something:

Examples:

- The student achieved high grades ***through*** hard work and study.

- The woman was overcharged for her purchase ***through*** a computer error.

Through is used to express the means by which something happens:

Examples:

- We got the information ***through*** his website.

- I got the job ***through*** an employment agency.

Throughout

Throughout is used to express that something is occurring everywhere, in all parts of:

Examples:

- There are yoga centers ***throughout*** New York City.

- There are fire alarm boxes ***throughout*** the building.

Throughout is used to talk about something occurring during an entire period of time:

Examples:

- He has been a very successful person ***throughout*** his life.
- We ask that students remain silent ***throughout*** the exam.
- We partied ***throughout*** the whole Christmas holiday.

To

To is used to indicate a response or reaction to something or someone:

Examples:

- I hope you will agree ***to*** my offer.
- The teacher hoped that the students paid attention ***to*** the lesson.
- Her reaction ***to*** that comment was negative.
- The old man was grateful ***to*** receive the help.

To is used to indicate a destination:

Examples:

- The plane ***to*** L.A. will arrive at 5 a.m..
- She wants sail ***to*** the South Pacific.
- The letter was ***to*** her.
- The sisters go ***to*** school every day, five days a week.

To is used to talk about time:

Examples:

- We work from 9 a.m. ***to*** 5 p.m. every day.
- They worked on the project from morning ***to*** night.

*Here is another way **to** is used to talk about time:*

- The time is now 15 minutes ***to*** 6. (a quarter to six)
- It's 20 minutes ***to*** noon.

To is used to help express who or what receives something; meaning, beneficiary of something:

Examples:

- His company awarded the prize ***to*** him for his hard work.
- The city dedicated the monument ***to*** the memory of its famous writer.
- The school gave a scholarship ***to*** the student because of her good work.

To is used to help express transferring and exchanging something from a person or a place:

Examples:

- The secretary brings the mail ***to*** the office every day.
- The student read his presentation ***to*** the class.

- The hair dresser recommended the hair conditioner *to* the woman.
- "Would you please give that *to* me," said Oliver Hardy to Stan Laurel. "Thank you."

To is used to help express what effect someone or something has on someone or something else:

Examples:

- Please stop having loud parties every night! You are a nuisance *to* the neighborhood. (And, besides, you never invite me.)
- The new park has been a pleasing experience *to* everyone.
- To my embarrassment, I sent the email *to* the wrong person.

To can be used to refer to one's self in a sentence:

Examples:

- *To* her disappointment, she didn't get a good grade on the final exam.
- The work was completed *to* their satisfaction.

To is used to help express repetition:

Examples:

- Our boat trip across the bay was really uncomfortable. The boat rolled side _**to**_ side.
- The homeless man went from house _**to**_ house asking for food.

_**To**_ is used to help express attaching something to something, or attachment:

Examples:

- She stapled the picture _**to**_ the form.
- The carpenter nailed the wood _**to**_ the floor.

_**To**_ is used to help express comparison:

Examples:

- The sun is very bright here, compared _**to**_ where I live.
- Your essay is very similar _**to**_ mine.

_**To**_ is used to indicate action caused by sound:

Examples:

- The next morning they woke up _**to**_ the sound of the ocean.
- She tapped her fingers _**to**_ the sound of the music.

_**To**_ is used to help express relationship of one thing to another:

Examples:

- I'd like to introduce you to the new assistant _to_ the director.

- These are the keys _to_ my car. Please don't crash it.

- The school building is close _to_ the mall.

- This street runs parallel _to_ that one.

- There are 3.8 liters _to_ one gallon.

_To_ is used to help express extremes:

Examples:

- She was so mad that she tore the contract _to_ bits.

- I'm trying to study and the noise from the party next door is driving me _to_ madness.

_To_ is used to help indicate problems or solutions:

Examples:

- Our water reservoirs are almost dry. This is a threat _to_ our survival.

- What is your solution _to_ this problem?

_To_ is used to help express ownership or connectedness:

Examples:

- That house belongs _**to**_ me.
- This issue is important _**to**_ me.
- He is married _**to**_ that woman.

_**To**_ is used to help express restrictedness:

Examples:

- The teenager was confined _**to**_ her room for disobeying her mother.
- The prisoners were restricted _**to**_ two meals a day.

Please refer to Focus On English, "Mastering English Gerunds and Infinitives", for more uses of the word **to**. There are also many other uses for the word **to** in English phrasal verbs and in English expressions (or idioms). Please refer to our book "Beyond Phrasal Verbs".

Toward(s)

**Toward(s)** is used to help express the direction to a location or place:

Examples:

- The tourists headed _**toward**_ the beach.
- We sailed our boat _**toward**_ the island.
- How do I find the iPod store?
  To find the iPod store, walk _**towards**_ the bank

for about 5 minutes, and then look to your left. It's the third store past the bank.

- The plane took off and headed **_toward_** Paris, France.

- See, over there. Look **_towards_** the intersection. You can see a man playing music on the street corner and dancing in his bare feet.

Toward(s) is used to help express contribution or making a partial payment:

Examples:

- The couple made a contribution of $1,000 **_towards_** the sick man's medical bills.

- The boy pays $50 every month **_towards_** his car payment.

Toward(s) is used to help express nearness to a certain time:

Examples:

- We always get excited about going skiing **_towards_** the middle of the winter.

- The math student was getting nervous **_towards_** the end of the exam because time was running out.

Toward(s) is used to help express attitude:

Examples:

- The parents are very loving ***towards*** their children.

- The students were very respectful ***towards*** their teacher.

Toward(s) is used to help express movement in the direction of some kind of action:

Examples:

- They are working ***towards*** an agreement.

- Peter is heading ***towards*** a decision to leave the company.

Chapter 5 <u>review</u>

Prepositions beginning with the letters $\underline{P} - \underline{T}$

*Instructions: read the sentences below. Decide whether the use of the preposition is correct or incorrect. If incorrect, which of these prepositions **best** fits the sentence: **<u>past</u>**, **<u>since</u>**, **<u>through</u>**, **<u>throughout</u>**, **<u>to</u>**, **<u>towards</u>**. The answers can be found at the bottom of the page.*

1. I haven't been in Tokyo **<u>since</u>** 1999. ☐correct ☐incorrect

2. The students passed **<u>through</u>** the museum and looked at the works of art. ☐correct ☐incorrect

3. There were many questions **<u>throughout</u>** the company meeting. ☐correct ☐incorrect

4. The student was grateful **<u>to</u>** receive tutoring from the teacher. ☐correct ☐incorrect

5. As soon as we got to Hawaii we headed **<u>since</u>** the beach. ☐correct ☐incorrect

6. Barbara is married **<u>past</u>** Alex Smith. ☐correct ☐incorrect

7. Our group sang songs **<u>throughout</u>** the train journey. ☐correct ☐incorrect

8. Every time I walk ***past*** the pastry shop I get hungry. ☐correct ☐incorrect

9. We attend school Monday ***through*** Friday every week. ☐correct ☐incorrect

10. The leader of the country has been kind ***to*** everyone.   ☐correct ☐incorrect

Answers: (1) correct; (2) correct; (3) correct; (4) correct; (5) incorrect; should be to; (6) incorrect; should be to; (7) correct; (8) correct; (9) correct; (10) correct

Chapter 6 - English prepositions beginning with the letters U - Z

This is a comprehensive listing of the most common English prepositions beginning with the letters _U_ - _Z_. The prepositions are followed by a usage explanation. After each explanation there are examples to help reinforce the correct use of the preposition in common English sentences.

Common English prepositions beginning with the letters U - Z

Below we will discuss these commonly used prepositions and provide you with many examples.

Under

Under is used to mean being in a lower position than, or beneath something or someone else:

Examples:

- The pen is **_under_** the table.
- The man is walking **_under_** the bridge.
- The submarine can travel **_under_** water.

Under is used to help express being under the supervision of or control of something or someone:

Examples:

- She has been very sick. Currently, she is **_under_** the supervision of a doctor.

- We are working **_under_** a manager that does not give us very much freedom.

- That country continues to suffer **_under_** bad leadership.

Under is used to express less than:

Examples:

- You can buy that car for **_under_** $20,000.

- Sorry, we can't sell you beer because you are **_under_** age 21.

Under can mean the same as **underneath** meaning hidden or covered by something else:

Examples:

- The cats hid **_under_** the house. We couldn't find them for days.

- She hid her purse **_under_** the bed.

- Sand crabs are found **_underneath_** the sand at the beach.

- He found his driver's license **_underneath_** a pile of papers on his desk.

Under can be used to express a situation, condition or state:

Examples:

- The website is **_under_** construction and should be done next month.

- The man was sent to jail for causing trouble while **_under_** the influence of alcohol.

Under can be used to identify categories:

Examples:

- You can find her name in the directory **_under_** the letter P.

- Porpoises can be found in the encyclopedia **_under_** mammals.

Underneath

Underneath is used to help express when something is being hidden or covered by something else:

Examples:

- **_Underneath_** her jacket she wore a sweater.

- I was very warm and cozy **_underneath_** the blankets of my bed.

Until

Until helps to express the beginning or end of an action, activity, situation or time:

Examples:

- I'm sorry sir, but the bank is closed. You will not be able to withdraw money ***until*** tomorrow.

- (Students taking an exam): Please do not leave your seats ***until*** the teacher gives you permission.

Up

Up can mean movement to a higher place:

Examples:

- The price of gasoline has really gone ***up***.
- The champagne cork flew ***up*** into the air when it was removed.

Up can be used to express movement against a current of water:

Examples:

- Salmon always swim ***up*** stream.

  Meaning: against the current of a river or stream
- We rowed the canoe ***up*** the river.

Up can be used to express forward movement towards a location further away:

Examples:

- The new park is **up** the road about ten miles and on your right.
- The bikers rode **up** the bike trail another five miles before they stopped and rested.

Up can be used to express forward movement along a route or path:

Examples:

- The truck traveled **up** the road.
- The two friends jogged **up** the path.

Up can be used to express division or cutting of something into pieces:

Examples:

- My mother chopped **up** the onion and then chopped **up** some garlic and put all the pieces in the sauce.
- The bank robbers divided **up** the money and then ran away.

*There are also many other uses for the word **up** in English phrasal verbs and in English expressions (or idioms). Please refer to our book, "Beyond Phrasal Verbs".*

Upon

Upon can be used in many of the same situations where <u>on</u> can be used:

Examples:

- **_Upon_** entering the room, everyone yelled, "surprise!"

- The stone was resting **_upon_** two supports

With

With can be used to express things being added on:

Examples:
- I like my tea **_with_** milk.

- How much is a hamburger **_with_** French fries.

With is used to express being together or in the company of:

Examples:
- I went **_with_** my brother to see the show.

- The students went **_with_** their teacher to the student auditorium.

- Did you see a man **_with_** a small boy within the last hour?

- Sally came to the party **_with_** her friend.

- Did you go _**with**_ her?

**With** is used to express a type of behavior:

Examples:
- They accepted the new jobs _**with**_ gratitude.
- Children have to be handled _**with**_ care.
- The teacher congratulated the class _**with**_ pride.
- The girl was being honest _**with**_ her friend.

**With** is used to help **ex**press feelings:

Examples:
- The office worker was bored _**with**_ her job.
- The newly wed couple were filled _**with**_ joy to be moving into a new home.

**With** is used to help express affiliation or relationship:

Examples:
- He has been working _**with**_ the International Red Cross for two years.
- Melissa works _**with**_ blind children.

**With** is used to help express conflict or struggle:

Examples:
- The children are always arguing _**with**_ each other.

- Our football team is going to compete *with* the champion team next week.

- He had trouble *with* the car. The motor wouldn't start.

With is used to help express filling or covering something or an area:

Examples:

- The waitress filled the glass *with* water.

- The whole side of the mountain was covered *with* wild flowers.

With helps to express which tool or implement is used to accomplish an action:

Examples:

- The artist painted a picture of the flower *with* his paintbrush.

- The worker dug a hole in the ground *with* a shovel.

With helps to express simultaneous (occurring together at the same time) time and direction:

Examples:

- The teacher always starts the class *with* a quiz.

- The monks always start their day *with* prayer.

- The boat sailed *with* the current.

__With__ helps to express parting or separation:

Examples:

- Toshiko is finished *__with__* her company and is now looking for a new job.

- She broke up *__with__* her boyfriend because they didn't spend enough time together.

__With__ helps to express cooperation:

Examples:

- All of the neighbors helped *__with__* cleaning the park.

- We decided to work *__with__* them on this important project.

- The car company has decided to form a partnership *__with__* their main parts manufacturer.

- We no longer do business *__with__* them.

__With__ helps to express comparisons:

Examples:

- Stefan's shirt didn't go *__with__* his pants.

  (Meaning: the colors of his shirt didn't look good *__with__* the color of his pants.)

- The value of the U.S. dollar is comparable *__with__* the value of the Canadian dollar.

  (Meaning: they are approximately equal in value.)

- Two different stores have the computer we want. We should compare one price **_with_** the other before we buy the computer.

With helps to express reason or cause:

Examples:
- The graduates were smiling **_with_** joy.
- The man was trembling **_with_** fear.

*There are other uses for the word **_with_** in English phrasal verbs and in English expressions (or idioms). Please refer to our book "Beyond Phrasal Verbs".*

Within

Within usually means inside of some area:

Examples:
- **_Within_** the room there were many fine paintings.
- **_Within_** the United States there are many fine universities.

Within can be used to express less than a specified period of time:

Examples:
- We should be finished **_within_** the hour.

- The bus usually comes **_within_** 15 minutes of the last bus. (☞ Meaning: in less than 15 minutes after the last bus left.)

Within can be used to express less than a specified distance:

Examples:

- The library is **_within_** two miles of the university.
- We are **_within_** two miles of our destination.

Without

Without can mean not having:

Examples:

- She gets to school **_without_** a car. She walks.
- **_Without_** your help, I couldn't have finished the project.
- **_Without_** water, we would not be able to live long.

Without can be used to express the absence of someone or something:

Examples:

- The worker finished the project **_without_** his colleagues.

- The baby tiger won't survive long ***without*** its mother.

Without can be used to express the absence of action:

Examples:

- He received a lot of money ***without*** working.
- She is famous ***without*** doing anything extraordinary.

Chapter 6 review *Prepositions beginning with the letters **P** – **T***

*Instructions: read the sentences below. Decide whether the use of the preposition is correct or incorrect. If incorrect, which of these prepositions **best** fits the sentence: **under**, **underneath**, **until**, **up**, **with**, **within**, **without**. The answers can be found on the bottom of the practice.*

1. Prices of food have really gone <u>up</u> ☐correct ☐incorrect

2. The boats were sailing <u>upon</u> the water. ☐correct ☐incorrect

3. The teacher worked <u>with</u> students to help them understand the new chapter. ☐correct ☐incorrect

4. My friend arrived home <u>with</u> her groceries. I helped my friend <u>until</u> her groceries. ☐correct ☐incorrect

5. <u>Without</u> the help of my family, I could never have finished school. ☐correct ☐incorrect

6. We won't complete the project <u>with</u> next Wednesday. ☐correct ☐incorrect

7. Our bus traveled <u>up</u> the highway at high speed. ☐correct ☐incorrect

8. The water passes <u>under</u> the bridge. ☐correct ☐incorrect

9. Alice bought the car for <u>under</u> $30,000. ☐correct ☐incorrect

10. She repaired her car <u>without</u> the help of her brothers. ☐correct ☐incorrect

Answers: (1) correct; (2) correct; (3) correct; (4) correct; (5) incorrect; should be <u>to;</u> (6) incorrect; should be <u>to;</u> (7) correct; (8) correct; (9) correct; (10) correct

Appendix; Quick-Find Menu

Prepositions following certain common English verbs, by <u>preposition.</u>

From

In

into

Of

To

About the Author

Thomas Celentano has written seven books about English grammar for English students worldwide and has taught English as a second language for more than 17 years. He holds university degrees in foreign language studies and anthropology from the University of Hawaii, at Manoa. He is also the author, under a pen name, of two novels and a book on natural healing.

Made in the USA
Columbia, SC
22 February 2021

33381823R00136